THE AMBASSADOR'S CALL

Gregory Addie

THE AMBASSADOR'S CALL

TRUE STORIES, ALLEGORIES & MIRACULOUS MEMOIRS

GREGORY ADDIE

The Ambassador's Call by Gregory Addie
Copyright © 2020 by Gregory Addie
All Rights Reserved.
ISBN: 978-1-59755-555-5

Published by: ADVANTAGE BOOKS™
　　　　　　　Longwood, Florida, USA
　　　　　　　www.advbookstore.com

This book and parts thereof may not be reproduced in any form, stored in a retrieval system or transmitted in any form by any means (electronic, mechanical, photocopy, recording or otherwise) without prior written permission of the author, except as provided by United States of America copyright law.

Unless otherwise indicated, all Scripture quotations are taken from the HOLY BIBLE, New King James Version®. Copyright © 1982 by Thomas Nelson, Inc. Used by permission. All rights reserved.

Scripture marked NIV are from the HOLY BIBLE, NEW INTERNATIONAL VERSION®. Copyright © 1973, 1978, 1984 Biblica. Used by permission of Zondervan. All rights reserved. The "NIV" and "New International Version" trademarks are registered in the United States Patent and Trademark Office by Biblica.

Scripture quotations marked KJV are from the HOLLY BIBLE, King James Version. Public domain.

Library of Congress Catalog Number: 2019957981

REL012040 RELIGION/ Christian Living / Inspirational

First Printing: January 2020
20 21 22 23 24 25 26   10 9 8 7 6 5 4 3 2 1
Printed in the United States of America

Table of Contents

CHAPTER 1: THE DIVER 7
- THE DIVER'S ALLEGORICAL MEANINGS DISCLOSED 10
- GOD'S MERCY REVEALED 16
- THE CONVERSION PROCESS BEGINS 17

CHAPTER 2: HEAVENLY CONFIRMATION 21
- ROMANS 10:13 21
- INTRODUCTION TO THE TRIUNE GOD 24
- PART 1 – THE NEW JERUSALEM 25
- PART TWO - THE STAGE IS SET 29
- THE FLYING SCROLL 34
- PART THREE - THE OFFERING 36
- YOU'RE NEXT 37

CHAPTER 3: SO IT BEGINS 41
- GRAMPA REX ON THE BANANA PEEL 41
- BARRENNESS TO BLESSING 45
- DEMONIC RESISTANCE 47
- DEMONIC HARASSMENT 49
- MOVING ON 53
- A TIME OF REVIEW 54

CHAPTER 4: BREANNA 55
- THE SACRIFICE 55
- THE STING 58
- A NEW CREATION 63
- GOD'S HUMOR 67

CHAPTER 5: GOD'S REPRESENTATIVE "THE AMBASSADOR" 69
- WALKING OUT THE AMBASSADOR CALLING 70
- CRUSADE FOR CHRIST 71
- A DOG NAMED REX 73

WHEN PHYSICAL HEALTH IS NOT DESIRED	75
A REPEAT CONFIRMATION	77
OUR ULTIMATE HEALING	78
WILD BULL	79
A FACEBOOK CHALLENGE	83
FILL 'R UP	85
THE JUDGMENT SEAT OF CHRIST	88
THE GREAT WHITE THRONE JUDGEMENT	90
THE BURNING HOUSE	91
THE MESSAGE	96
THE HOLY SPIRIT'S INEXHAUSTIBLE WORKS	97
CHAPTER 6: GOING FOR THE GOLD	**101**
INSIGHTS INTO GOING FOR THE GOLD ALLEGORY	104
THE ALLEGORY EXPLAINED	106
THE LOTTERY TICKET	108
THE SECOND LOTTERY TICKET	111
CHAPTER 7: THE HORSE AND RIDER	**115**
THE ALLEGORY EXPLAINED	118
OUR INITIAL JOURNEY	119
THROUGH THE YEARS	120
OUR PERCEIVED FALL AND FAILURES	121
THE RIDER'S RESCUE	121
CHAPTER 8: THE TRAIN STATION	**125**
THE GATHERING	126
THE ARRIVAL	129
THE DEPARTURE	132
THE END IS JUST THE BEGINNING	132
A SALVATION PRAYER	135
FUTURE WRITINGS IN THE WORKS	**136**

Chapter 1

The Diver

On a distant seashore a young man prepares for an adventure. He stands on a white sand beach with a picturesque lighthouse high on a hill. With his wetsuit on and his air tank secure, he finishes his checklist for the deep dive for which he is nearly ready to embark.

"Weight belt. Check. Diving knife. Check. Timing watch. Check. Mask. Check. Fins. Check. Underwater flares for light. Check." Now he is ready to launch his boat into the unknown adventure that lies beneath the sea before him.

He casts off and steers his boat in the direction of a coral reef. As he glides toward his dive point, he notes and then ignores a floating buoy with a warning sign which says, "**Unexplored Reef Area - Dive at Your Own Risk**." He thinks to himself, "Unexplored, aye. *I* will be the first to dive this section. Surely, they will name it after my explorations are completed and I disclose all this reef's secrets."

His imagination runs wild with thoughts of potential treasures of old waiting on the bottom of the sea floor - perhaps gold coins, ancient artifacts or even unknown sea life yet to be named are waiting just for him. Like Adam in the Garden of Eden, he boldly continues to claim and name his section of the reef in his mind.

However, a sense of caution tugs at his gut as he hears the voices of other mature divers many years ago cautioning him to never dive alone. Those voices whisper through his mind as he considers the "What ifs" of his dive. "What if I get into trouble down there?" echoes back at him. "I am alone on this dive and would have no one to help me if trouble occurs."

The diver quickly dismisses the fear gnawing at the back of his mind and muses, "It is a beautiful sunny day. What could possibly go wrong?" He looks intently into the water and thinks, "Clear as crystal. This should be the perfect spot." He anchors his boat, jumps into the water and begins to observe his surroundings.

The sun's light magnifies the beauty of the multicolored reef. Aquatic life is everywhere. The water is warm and caresses the diver's tense reflexes urging relaxation.

"I could stay here for hours," he thinks but then remembers he only has so much air in his tank. He checks his air watch. "Good. Plenty of time," he says to himself.

With "plenty of time to explore" on his mind and more adrenaline than air, he utters these words, "Go boldly now where no man has gone before!" Like a fictitious Captain Kirk, he dives forward as if to board the Starship Enterprise and begins his descent down the coral reef.

As the diver goes deeper, he notes that the sun's light is somewhat dimmer. There is a chill in the water and all the glorious beauty seen near the surface has all but disappeared. He looks beneath him and sees that it is even darker in the depths. He sees a faint outline of what appears to be the mast of a sunken ship.

"GO FOR IT, KIRK," resounds in his mind. With a 'full steam ahead' approach, he lights a flare and continues his descent down into the cold dark depths. As he reaches the bottom his flare's light illuminates not just one ship but a vast graveyard of ships. "Did they not see the lighthouse up on the hill?" he wonders. "How foolish of them not to heed its light during the night."

As he gazes at the shipwrecks, he notices an opening to a cave at the bottom of the reef. "Now this is what I'm talking about," he thinks to himself. With his flare still glowing he enters the wide mouth of the cave and begins to explore.

The walls of the cave glisten with unknown minerals that seem to beckon him into further adventure. As he glides forward, he finds that one tunnel splits into other tunnels. Confusion begins to set in as still more tunnels appear to go in a vast number of directions. Choosing one, he swims his way into an open cavern.

Realizing his flare is nearly spent, he lights another and it brightly illuminates the cavern walls which are also impregnated with reflective minerals. As the cavern fills with light he sees that he is not alone. For inside this cavern are a dozen other divers who had previously explored this reef. Their lifeless multicolored wetsuits are firmly anchored to the cave floor by their leaded weight belts.

Suddenly, a wave of fear washes over him as he recalls reading in the widely published *Divers' Digest* about obeying diving warning signs like the one on the buoy he saw when he started out. He also recalls that the *Divers' Digest* reported in several different editions about many divers never being found in areas that were posted by the buoys.

Like a drowning rat, he turns to leave the cavern at the same time as his air's timing watch begins vibrating on his wrist, signaling that he has only five minutes of air left. The diver stares at his vibrating watch and realizes he has been in the depths too long! He must return to the surface or die like the divers before him. With great anxiety, he attempts to locate the main tunnel he came through to enter the cavern. However, his panicked exit attempt has now stirred up the cavern's sediment floor debris throughout the water around him and, as the debris swirls, it blinds his escape.

"I will never make it out!" his mind screams as his diving watch once again vibrates, this time with a two-minute warning reminding him that his air is about to run out and his time below the surface is about to expire.

"How could I be so stupid, so naïve, so careless?" His thoughts of adventure now dim inside him as he realizes the stark reality at hand. Fully grasping his outcome, the diver reaches for his diving knife. "Others," he thinks, "Might venture down into this cavern and must be told my story."

With his flare beginning to flicker, the diver begins carving a final statement into the cavern wall with his knife. He writes:

"The beauty was there, so I took the dare. I now am lost and I must pay the cost."

His last words written, the flare gives up its light. The diver is all alone now in his self-imposed darkness. Hopelessly, he slumps down onto the floor of the cavern as his timing watch vibrates its final call. He closes his eyes and waits for his last breath.

Above him the sun's light is setting and it begins to highlight other areas on the surface of the coral reef. Below, the diver senses light on his eyelids. He opens his eyes to see that the lifeless divers' bloated multicolored wetsuits are glowing fluorescently in this light from above. With a last-ditch effort and a glimmer of hope, the diver makes his way along the cavern floor to where he can see a shaft of light exposing a narrow opening in the cavern ceiling.

With his lungs burning for oxygen, he pushes upward and attempts to make his way through the opening only to find his wetsuit and equipment will not fit. He quickly sheds his weight belt, air tank, mask and knife. With great effort he struggles through the narrow passage. He bursts through the surface of the water and gasps for air like a baby who has just left the womb to be born.

The last of the daylight has disappeared now and the diver treads water in the darkness searching for his way home. Out of the corner of his eye he catches a flash skimming off the water. He turns and faces the direction of the flash. High on the hill in the distance the old faithful lighthouse shines its beam onto his face. He weeps in relief as he swims back to shore where safety and rescue await him.

The Diver's Allegorical Meanings Disclosed

This allegorical story may have different meanings for different readers but because this book is my own memoir, I am using the story of the diver to illustrate how I came to know Jesus Christ and what methods were employed by God to create a new heart inside me.

Like a piece of pottery hardened by time, a potter must sometimes allow his work to be crushed into fine dust. From there he can apply water and reform the clay (or one's heart) into a new creation by the finesse of the potter's hand.

We see this in several scripture verses:

> ***Isaiah 64:8. But now, O Lord, You are our Father; We are the clay, and You are our potter; And we all are the work of Your hand.***
>
> ***Jeremiah 18:4. And the vessel that he made of clay was marred in the hand of the potter; so he made it again into another vessel, as it seemed good to the potter to make.***
>
> ***Romans 9:21. Does not the potter have power over the clay, from the same lump to make one vessel for honor and another for dishonor?***

So, the diver in this story is an allegory of the relational LOVE of God toward one of His human creations, namely "myself". The diver was a young man entering the great sea of youthful adventure and relational love. Being young, he thought he possessed all the material necessities to enter into this deep unexplored area. To the diver and myself, it was just a physical undertaking that took external skill, but I did not realize it was a common error of most unlearned young men to embark on this trip alone.

At this time in my life I was 24 years old and thought I had the world by the tail. I had a prestigious job, plenty of spendable cash, a new vehicle and a carefree attitude that meant 'anything goes' that catered to my glutinous material lifestyle. The only thing missing was a centerpiece called a wife.

Arrogantly, I thought of myself as a well-fit good looking young man at 6'3" with blue eyes and, having recently been honorably discharged from the Marine Corps, I was athletic, always being one of the first picks onto the basketball court because of my history as a high school varsity starter and skilled in self-defense martial arts.

My idiot self-thought I was a prize to be had for any woman. Little did my mind understand, nor do many other young men understand, that these attributes are some of the last things a young woman is looking for in a lifelong mate.

Like the diver, I jumped headfirst into the sea of relational and physical lovemaking. The diver saw upon his entry into the sea that it can be a beautiful place. The coral reef he observed with its sunlit beauty was much like I saw in my quest to fulfill this internal, yet natural drive for relational fulfillment. As the saying goes, "There are a lot of fish in the sea." The trick is finding the right one.

As the diver descended into the depths of exploration, the water became colder and the light became dimmer. This is like most of us as we realize that a loving relationship is not an instant reality. When we find that there is not even a possibility of it on the horizon, our heart becomes either hopeless, lonely, or hardened or a combination thereof. We see this in:

Proverbs 13:12 Hope deferred makes the heart sick, but when the desire comes, it is a tree of life.

As the diver reached the bottom of his descent, he noticed all the shipwrecks that lay on the sea floor. These shipwrecks represent the many relationships I had been through up to this point in my young life. From my first date at 15 to the age of 24, I had had at least a dozen shipwrecked relationships.

In the dating world I had found that most shallow relationships only lasted 3 to 6 months. Either I was dumping them or they were dumping me, but like the diver, I pressed on always thinking that the perfect relationship was out there to be had.

The cave's entrance in this story, that was not far from the shipwrecks, was for me the entrance into a relationship that I really thought would soon lead to marriage. When the relationship first began, everything about it was like the sparkling minerals on the cave's walls. However, I was soon to find out that this relationship, like all the other previous relationships I had had, was to have a similar time frame leading to its conclusion.

Just like the twists and turns inside the cave's tunnels, I found myself questioning the loyalty of my newly found female friend. You see, I knew upfront, that she was cohabitating with another gentleman but it didn't seem to matter to either of us. We both were magically in love or deceivingly infatuated with each another.

A popular song during the 1980s was "Jessie's Girl" by Rick Springfield. Since copyright law prohibits me from disclosing the entire lyrics, I can tell you the refrain rang out, "I WISH THAT I HAD JESSIE'S GIRL." You can listen to the song on YouTube if you want to understand my full motivation for this young woman. Every word in the lyrics mirrored my feelings for her. What was even worse was that "Jessie" was a friend of mine whom I was betraying behind his back.

Like the diver who saw the warning on the buoy and had wrestled with his thoughts on the way down to "**Not Proceed Any Farther**" and who had justified his actions, I had many of the same warnings speaking to my heart at that time. But, like the diver, I rationalized my actions and decided to just "GO FOR IT". Yes, Karma was about to have its full recourse with my betrayal of my friend.

The Bible speaks to our process of reasoning and how it gets us into trouble:

> ***James 1:13-15*** *[13] Let no one say when he is tempted, "I am tempted by God" for God cannot be tempted by evil, nor does He Himself tempt anyone.[14] But each one is tempted when he is drawn away by his own desires and enticed.[15] Then, when desire*

has conceived, it gives birth to sin; and sin, when it is full-grown, brings forth death.

There is another biblical passage that talks about these kinds of relationships and how one will end up at their conclusion. The passage reads as follows:

***Proverbs 7:6-27** ⁶For at the window of my house I looked through my lattice, ⁷and saw among the simple, I perceived among the youths, a young man devoid of understanding, ⁸passing along the street near her corner; and he took the path to her house ⁹In the twilight, in the evening, in the black and dark night. ¹⁰And there a woman met him, with the attire of a harlot and a crafty heart. ¹¹She was loud and rebellious; her feet would not stay at home. ¹²At times she was outside, at times in the open square, lurking at every corner. ¹³So she caught him and kissed him; with an impudent face she said to him: ¹⁴"I have peace offerings with me; today I have paid my vows. ¹⁵So I came out to meet you, diligently to seek your face, and I have found you. ¹⁶I have spread my bed with tapestry, colored coverings of Egyptian linen. ¹⁷I have perfumed my bed with myrrh, aloes and cinnamon. ¹⁸Come, let us take our fill of love until morning; let us delight ourselves with love. ¹⁹For my husband is not at home; he has gone on a long journey; ²⁰He has taken a bag of money with him, and will come home the appointed day. ²¹With her enticing speech she caused him to yield, with her flattering lips she seduced him. ²²Immediately he went after her, as an ox goes to the slaughter, or as a fool to the correction of the stocks, ²³until an arrow struck his liver. As a bird hastens to the snare, he did not know it would cost his life. ²⁴Now therefore, listen to me, my children; pay attention to the words of my mouth: ²⁵Do not let your heart turn aside to her ways, do not stray into her paths; ²⁶For she has cast down many wounded. And <u>all who</u>*

were slain by her were strong men. ²⁷Her house is the way to hell, descending to the chambers of death. (emphasis mine)

As the diver in this story came to the end of the tunnel and found himself inside an inescapable cavern, I found myself in the same "cavern," not being able to escape the emotional ties I had to this woman. The loss of closeness from our many intimate encounters, and her final decision to marry "Jessie" instead of me left me feeling helpless. Like so many women before her that had wanted marriage to me, I now found myself with the shoe on the other foot of relational rejection, disillusionment and loss. Just like the diver in the cavern whose time of fresh air had expired, I, too, on my heart's wall wrote the same farewell statement:

"The beauty was there so I took the dare. I now am lost and I must pay the cost."

I entered a state of hopelessness and depression just like the diver who sat down and waited for his end to come. It was all I could do to go to work and see her at her job. You see, part of my Karma was looking every day at someone I still loved but could never have. I remember coming home and just going to bed, not waking until it was time to go back to work, only to repeat the same agony of visual defeat. This went on for weeks and I began to sink deeper into a pit of depression from which I thought I could never escape.

Finally, she and her fiancé left this place of employment and got married. You might say **I** got left holding the bag this time. Normally it was some other person's heart that was left holding the bag.

I have used the word KARMA loosely in this story. Karma is a trending word that means the following:

"One of the basic teachings of Theosophy, Karma is the cosmic principle according to which each person is rewarded or punished in one incarnation according to that person's deeds in the previous incarnation."

Since I do not believe in incarnation, I will give you the biblical version of what I am saying:

> ***Galatians 6:7 Do not be deceived, God is not mocked; for whatever a man sows, that he will also reap.***

This verse does not say that God is handing out the payback. It is more like the natural law that says "for every action, there is an equal and opposite reaction."

God's Mercy Revealed

The diver in our story had reached a state of hopelessness and was just waiting inside the dark cavern for the inevitable. It was not until he saw the sunlight's final reflection that he was able to get a second chance.

For me, this time in my life was much like that diver being an introvert in a mentally dark place. What I did not know at the time is that there was a person out there praying some consistent big-time prayers to God for my heart to turn back to its childhood roots of faith and receive the salvation of God through Jesus Christ.

Prayer is a powerful tool that God gives people of faith; we see this in

> ***James 5:16 Confess your trespasses to one another, and pray for one another, that you may be healed. The effective, fervent prayer of a righteous man avails much.***

I know there may be a few of you reading this who are thinking, "he got exactly what he deserved." If God counted all our transgressions against us, who could ever stand the judgment we will face one day? We see this in:

> ***Psalm 130:3 If You, LORD, should mark iniquities, O Lord, who could stand?***

Also, His character toward us can be seen in these passages:

Psalm 86:15 But You, O Lord, are a God full of compassion, and gracious, Longsuffering and abundant in mercy and truth.

Psalm 34:18 The Lord is near to those who have a broken heart, and saves such as have a contrite spirit.

Psalm 51:17 The sacrifices of God are a broken spirit, a broken and a contrite heart — These, O God, You will not despise.

Isaiah 57:15 For thus says the High and Lofty One who inhabits eternity, whose name is Holy: "I dwell in the high and holy place, with him who has a contrite and humble spirit, to revive the spirit of the humble, and to revive the heart of the contrite ones.

Like our diver friend inside the dark cavern, I saw the light at the last moment and escaped after I confessed all my wrongdoings and brokenness to the Lord Jesus Christ. God, through Jesus Christ, invites all of us to escape this place of inner damnation. God says in:

Isaiah 1:16-18 16"Wash yourselves, make yourselves clean; put away the evil of your doings from before My eyes. Cease to do evil, 17Learn to do good; seek justice, rebuke the oppressor; defend the fatherless, plead for the widow. 18"Come now, and let us reason together," says the LORD, "Though your sins are like scarlet, They shall be as white as snow; Though they are red like crimson, They shall be as wool.

The Conversion Process Begins

My healing and coming back from the abyss would come from a time of childhood remembrance. There is a biblical verse that says in:

Proverbs 22:6 "Train up a child in the way he should go, and when he is old he will not depart from it."

My childhood learning about God began in a Catholic church, progressed to a protestant Free Methodist church and then finally to a protestant Nazarene church before I bailed into exploring the reefs of life on my own.

However, it was during my childhood that my Dad would take me with him to hear gospel quartets. During those concerts I would experience a "Peaceful Presence" that planted seeds of future recovery into my soul. I spent hours listening to gospel records by various groups just so I could re-experience the "Peaceful Presence" that the music would bring.

During this time of depression in my relational recovery, I VIVIDLY REMEMBER sitting on my bed one night sobbing when I began to sense this same "Peaceful Presence".

Like the diver trapped in the cavern saw the shaft of light, a light was beginning to shine into my heart via those old remembered gospel quartet experiences.

As I began to feel this "Peaceful Presence," a picture formed in my mind of a man standing at a crossroad. One direction was filled with darkness, barrenness, cloudiness and storms; the other direction was just a path where a light could be seen at its end.

It was then that I could hear a voice in my mind telling me to "choose" the path I would walk in the future. I then realized that it was **God** speaking to me and **He** wanted a decision from me concerning my life.

Out loud I answered the voice in my mind and said, "God, if this is You, I want You to take me down the path towards the light." Immediately after I spoke those words, the "Presence of Peace" filled my room a hundredfold and washed over me like a cleansing wave.

Just as the diver shed excess baggage, I shed every weight, care and hurt and made my way up through the narrow passage of depression into a breath of fresh air. There is a good biblical verse that describes the action I took that night in accepting God's path. It is found in:

> **Matthew 7:13-14** *13"Enter by the narrow gate; for wide is the gate and broad is the way that leads to destruction, and there are many who go in by it. 14Because narrow is the gate and difficult is the way which leads to life, and there are few who find it.*

The diver also, once he had shed all his securities and taken the narrow tunnel, came up above his circumstance and then found his way back home by looking toward the lighthouse beacon shining through the darkness. That night when I decided to go down the path toward the light, it was not necessarily a lifestyle change for me. Rather, it was a relationship change of giving up the old hurtful love of a human female and replacing it with the natural love of my Creator namely, Jesus Christ Himself. We see this in:

> **John 8:12** *When Jesus spoke again to the people, He said, "I am the light of the world. Whoever follows Me will never walk in darkness but will have the light of life."*

The next morning, I awoke in a much more rested fashion and I felt a BIRTH of LIFE inside me that would help me climb out of this pit of depression that had its hold on me.

As the days went by, I reflected on more of my childhood experiences within the protestant church which led me to this big question, "WAS I GOING TO HEAVEN SOME DAY?"

Now one would think that after having a life altering experience with God, one would already be assured of the answer to this eternal question. In the next chapter I will share an experience that blew all doubt of this AWAY!

Gregory Addie

Chapter 2

Heavenly Confirmation

Romans 10:13

Like what I had done just a few nights earlier, I spoke (or what we call prayed) to God about my earlier "Peaceful Presence" visitation.

I was determined to get clarification for myself that I ready did have a **"God Experience" and that Jesus Christ** was really the way to eternal salvation. I wanted to get down **to where the rubber meets the road** as far as being convinced.

At *this* point in my life I had gone through so many hurtful, heart wrenching, tear jerking, trust breaking relationships that I had taken *somewhat* of a biblical Doubting Thomas attitude. You remember good *old Thomas,* one of Jesus' *disciples* who had said in:

> *John 20:24 "Unless I see in His hands the print of the nails, and put my finger into the print of the nails, and put my hand into His side, I will not believe."*

Thomas would not believe Jesus was alive, let alone had been raised from the dead. Little did I know that I was about to get a Thomas **disciple wake up call** from God.

Before I went to bed one night I reached out to God. I PRAYED a simple prayer in which I simply asked God to show me in some way that my experience was real and that I would go to Heaven someday if I just believed in salvation through Jesus.

When I went to sleep that night, I had a dream where I was in a room with an old fashioned movie screen. Remember those? They were used to show reel-to-reel movies. The screen was still in its rolled up position and was not ready for use. A partial lower arm and hand appeared which was covered by a sleeve like that of a pure white garment. Then the hand took the screen and unrolled it into a usable position. Instantly, the screen was filled with a brilliant white light. Like in a 3D movie, far back in the screen there rolled a little round rock which began small and grew larger as it rolled closer to the front of the screen. It kept rolling forward like it was going to come right out of the screen at me.

Just before the now very large rock burst through the screen, it stopped abruptly. I could see an inscription stamped on the face of it which simply read **ROMANS 10:13**. This same scenario played itself out a total of three times and then I suddenly woke up.

I knew this must be in the Bible somewhere as I remembered going to a Free Methodist Church as a young teen and hearing things like this. The only Bible I had in my house at the time was a little green micro-print Gideons New Testament Bible that I had received as part of my field gear when I joined the United States Marine Corps.

Now wide awake, I got up out of bed and dug the miniature Bible out of my old Marine Corp duffle bag and fumbled my way through the table of contents to find that indeed there was a book called Romans in the Bible. I turned to it, found the chapter and verse and here's how it read:

Romans 10:13 For "whoever calls on the name of the Lord shall be saved."

Talk about a direct answer from God on that little prayer request I had made before going to bed that night! **WOW**! **God** had spoken to **me**! I began to get really excited, but most of all I began to have

FAITH that there truly was a God and this part about Jesus **must** be true.

In hindsight, I am still amazed and quite humbled that the **God of the universe,** who has millions of prayers thrown at Him constantly, would be kind enough to take the time to answer **my** prayer in such a personal way. I believe that God in His wisdom was beginning to introduce me to this book called the BIBLE.

Now just for clarity, I would like to put this in context with the verses that precede *Romans 10:13* and, for those of you who may just be beginning to reason out this Jesus thing, I am including:

> *Romans 10:8-13* *⁸But what does it say? "The word is near you, in your mouth and in your heart" (that is, the word of faith which we preach): ⁹that if you <u>confess</u> with your mouth the Lord Jesus and <u>believe</u> in your heart that God has raised Him from the dead, <u>you will be saved</u>. ¹⁰For with the heart one believes unto righteousness, and with the mouth confession is made unto salvation. ¹¹For the Scripture says, "Whoever believes on Him will not be put to shame." ¹²For there is no distinction between Jew or Greek, for the same Lord over all is rich to all who call upon Him. ¹³For "<u>whoever calls upon the name of the Lord shall be saved.</u>" (emphasis mine)*

As a side note, I realized while writing this book that God tends to speak in *threes* as He showed me in my dream and the apostle Paul wrote in:

> *Acts 10:15-16. ¹⁵nd a voice spoke to him again the second time, "What God has cleansed, you must not call common." ¹⁶This was done <u>three times</u>. And the object was taken up into heaven again. (emphasis mine)*

Introduction to the Triune God

A few weeks after I had the **Romans 10:13** experience, I had an unsolicited dream that would really become a "Salvation Clincher" and would "seal the deal" in my faith in Jesus Christ forever.

I had just finished another third shift at the food processing plant where I worked and was about to go to bed. That morning, I had felt like kneeling for a brief minute to thank God for accepting me in the supernatural way that He had done.

Mind you, during this time, I was still wrestling with my emotions over my broken heart from my previous relationship with the woman I thought I was going to marry. A broken heart, my friends, is not quickly mended. It takes time for your soul to heal after you have become one with someone physically, mentally and emotionally.

There is a biblical verse I would like to interject at this point that was recorded by Dr. Luke who wrote the Gospel called Luke. Jesus said:

> ***Luke 4:18** "The Spirit of the Lord is upon me, because He has anointed me to preach the gospel to the poor; He has SENT ME TO HEAL THE BROKENHEARTED, to proclaim liberty to the captives, and recovery of sight to the blind, to set at liberty those who are oppressed." (emphasis mine)*

I pray that this verse helps everyone reading this book who may fall into any of the above categories. There is good news for **all** of us who have been downtrodden in life. You see, the Bible also says in:

> ***Hebrews 13:8** Jesus Christ is the same yesterday, today, and forever."*

So what He does for one, He will do for **all** who call upon Him. THAT'S GOOD NEWS!

Before I reveal how this next three part dream played out, I want you to know I have had decades now to analyze the validity of this dream and to find Scripture references for it. So, as I go through these next three sections, I am going to parenthesize Scripture verses that are listed in their entirety at the end of each section. This will make reading the next sections much smoother as you discover the dream's hidden treasures and analytical meanings. OK, here we go.

Part 1 – The New Jerusalem

After I finished my nightly prayer time, I slipped into my warm water bed (folks, that really dates me, LOL). I soon fell asleep and began to dream another dream that was sure to change my soul forever. Suddenly I found myself standing in a brilliant green pasture (***Psalm 23:1-2***). Above me was a bright blue sky with no clouds in it to cast a shadow on the ground or shade an area (***Mark 4:22***). I must note here that as I had this dream, vision, or third heaven experience, the colors were clean, vivid and crisp to my sight. As I stood there the blue sky split open like a book about to share its secret story.

While gazing up into the sky, I sensed a loving Peaceful Presence behind me. It was the same Presence I had felt many other times as a boy at the altar, while listening to my Dad's gospel quartet records and just weeks before when I experienced the initial nighttime visitation while I was mentally falling apart as I lay upon my bed of woe.

A hand touched my shoulder. In the blink of an eye I was propelled from the green pasture up through the opening in the sky. It seemed as if I had crossed into another dimension of which we humans are oblivious while we live in this worldly dimension.

The first thing I observed was a scale model of a very large city under construction, very similar to what a human engineer creates to help one envision how a completed project will look. I went to the cornerstone of this scale model (***Matthew 21:42***, ***Acts 4:11-12***, ***Ephesians 2:20***) and the city's outer walls stretched as far as my eyes could see in one direction and the same in the other direction (***John 14:2-3, Revelation 21:9-27***).

This first part of the dream was really an introduction to a place that God is preparing for those who have given their lives over to the good news or the Gospel of Jesus Christ (***Revelation 21*** and ***Revelation 22:1- 5***).

What a relief it was to me to actually see that God was preparing a place for this guy named Gregory Addie. If this was all there was to the dream, it would have been enough; however, God was not done with me yet.

Scripture references for Part One:

> *Psalm 23:1-2 The Lord is my shepherd; I shall not want. ²He makes me lie down in <u>green pastures</u>; (emphasis mine)*

> *Mark 4:22 For there is <u>nothing hidden</u> which will not be revealed, nor has anything been kept secret but that it should come to light. (emphasis mine)*

> *Matthew 21:42 Jesus said to them, "Have you never read in the Scriptures, 'The stone which the builders rejected has become the chief <u>cornerstone</u>. This was the Lord's doing, and it is marvelous in our eyes'?' (emphasis mine)*

> *Acts 4:11-12 ¹¹This is the 'stone which was rejected by you builders, which has become the chief <u>cornerstone</u>.' ¹²Nor is there salvation in any other for there is no other name under heaven given among men by which we must be saved." (emphasis mine)*

> *Ephesians 2:20 Having been built on the foundation of the apostles and prophets, Jesus Christ Himself being the chief <u>cornerstone</u>, (emphasis mine)*

John 14:2-3 *²In My Father's house are many mansions; if it were not so, I would have told you. I go to prepare <u>a place for you</u>. ³And if I go and prepare a place for you, I will come again and receive you to Myself; that where I am, there you may be also. (emphasis mine)*

Revelation 21:1–8 Now I saw a new heaven and a new earth, for the first heaven and the first earth had passed away. Also there was no more sea. ²Then I, John, saw the holy city, New Jerusalem, coming down out of heaven from God prepared as a bride adorned for her husband. ³And I heard a loud voice from heaven saying, "Behold, the tabernacle of God is with men, and He will dwell with them, and they shall be His people. God Himself will be with them and be their God. ⁴And God will wipe away every tear from their eyes; there shall be no more death, nor sorrow, nor crying. There shall be no more pain, for the former things have passed away." ⁵Then He who sat on the throne said, "Behold, I make all things new." And He said to me, "Write, for these words are true and faithful." ⁶And He said to me, "It is done! I am the Alpha and the Omega, the Beginning and the End. I will give of the fountain of the water of life freely to him who thirsts. ⁷He who overcomes shall inherit all things, and I will be his God and he shall be My son. ⁸But the cowardly, unbelieving, abominable, murderers, sexually immoral, sorcerers, idolaters and all liars shall have their part in the lake which burns with fire and brimstone, which is the second death."

Revelation 21:9-27 ⁹Then one of the seven angels who had the seven bowls filled with the seven last plagues came to me and talked with me, saying, "Come, I will show you the bride, the Lamb's wife." ¹⁰And he carried me away in the Spirit to a great and high mountain, and showed me <u>the great city</u>, <u>the holy Jerusalem</u>, descending out of heaven from God, ¹¹having the glory of God. Her light was like a most precious stone, like a jasper stone, clear as crystal. ¹²Also she had <u>a great and high wall</u> with twelve gates, and twelve angels at the gates, and names written on them, which are the names of the twelve tribes of the children of Israel: ¹³three gates on the east, three gates on the north, three gates on the south, and three gates on the west. ¹⁴Now the wall of the city had twelve foundations, and on them were the names of the twelve apostles of the Lamb. ¹⁵And he who talked with me had a gold reed to measure the city, its gates, and its wall. ¹⁶The city is laid out as a square; its length is as great as its breadth. And he measured the city with the reed: <u>twelve thousand furlongs</u>. Its length, breadth, and height are equal. ¹⁷Then he measured its <u>wall: one hundred and forty-four cubits</u>, according to the measure of a man, that is, of an angel. ¹⁸The construction of its wall was of jasper; and the city was pure gold, like clear glass. ¹⁹The foundations of the wall of the city were adorned with all kinds of precious stones: the first foundation was jasper, the second sapphire, the third chalcedony, the fourth emerald, ²⁰the fifth sardonyx, the sixth sardius, the seventh chrysolite, the eighth beryl, the ninth topaz, the tenth chrysoprase, the eleventh jacinth, and the twelfth amethyst. ²¹The twelve gates were twelve pearls: each individual gate was of one pearl. And the street of the city was pure gold, like transparent glass. ²²But I saw no temple in it, for the Lord God Almighty and the Lamb are its temple. ²³The city had no need of the sun or of the moon to shine in it, for the glory of God illuminated it. The Lamb is its light. ²⁴And the nations of those who are saved shall walk in its light, and the kings of the earth bring their glory and honor into it. ²⁵Its gates shall not be shut at all by day (there shall be no night there). ²⁶ And they shall bring the glory and the honor of the nations into it. ²⁷But there shall by no means enter it anything that defiles, or *causes an abomination or a lie, but only those who are written in the Lamb's Book of Life. (emphasis mine)*

Revelation 22:1-5 And he showed me a pure river of water of life, clear as crystal, proceeding from the throne of God and of the Lamb. [2]In the middle of its street, and on either side of the river, was the tree of life, which bore twelve fruits, each tree yielding its fruit every month. The leaves of the tree were for the healing of the nations. [3]And there shall be no more curse, but the throne of God and of the Lamb shall be in it, and His servants shall serve Him. [4]They shall see His face, and His name shall be on their foreheads. [5]There shall be no night there: They need no lamp nor light of the sun, for the Lord God gives them light. And they shall reign forever and ever.

Part Two - The Stage Is Set

In a nanosecond my observation changed from the scale model of the city being built to a room that appeared to be an auditorium with a gigantic stage. I found myself standing in the upper rear of this room. The floor sloped down to an elevated stage which was recessed into the back wall of the structure. The stage was framed by a crimson red velvet curtain that draped onto the floor.

Standing in front of and to the right-hand side of the stage were multitudes of translucent people. I sensed that these were the spirits of people who had died and no longer had their physical fleshly bodies (*2 Corinthians 5:1-8*). They stood there silently, apparently waiting for someone or something to come onto the stage. To the left of the stage there was nothing but empty space (*Matthew 25:31-46*).

Suddenly, there was Jesus Christ in the flesh walking onto the stage. I say "in the flesh" because I could see the veins on the side of His neck and they were just like those of a man. A name rumbled through my mind - "The God Man – Christ Jesus." He wore a garment of white and His hair was not like most illustrations depict

Him. Instead, it was purest white and looked more like finely groomed snow.

Jesus looked across the platform at all the translucent people. With outstretched arms, He raised both His hands above His head and said, "ALL PRAISE THE FATHER." In unison the translucent people began praising God the Father in a heavenly language that I still do not fully understand. It seemed that it was part song and part words in what many Pentecostals would call "tongues."

As I write this I recall:

John 4:23 "Yet a time is coming and has now come when the true worshipers will worship the Father in the Spirit and in truth, for they are the kind of worshipers the Father seeks."

As they were praising God the Father, an unseen Presence filled the room. This Presence, to my understanding, was God the Father, Who is Spirit. Like a tidal wave of joy, peace, and glory, His Presence entered the room encompassing these His people with His accepting love. His loving and peaceful Presence was a thousand times more intense than anything else I had experienced up to this point in my life. It was like a million meaningful embraces wrapped around me and given in a split second of time. Suddenly, I was moved closer to the stage by the same hand on my shoulder that I had felt when I was in the green pasture.

Years later I would realize that God was introducing me to the Holy Trinity in this place. The One with His hand on my shoulder was the third person of the Trinity, the Holy Spirit, who the Scriptures said (***John 16:5-15***) would be our Guide and Comforter. Of course, the God Man - Jesus Christ is the second person of the Trinity and God the Father is the first person of the Trinity. As a new Christian, this dream was burnt into me so that I would never accept any of the numerous false religions in our world today.

By this time, I had reached the front edge of the stage. I was closer now in body to Jesus than I had ever been and the closer I got the more intense was the glory and love radiating from His being, so much so that I fell like a dead man, much like the apostle John did on the island of Patmos when he received the vision he described in the Book of Revelation (***Revelation 1:17-18)***.

I began to weep uncontrollably. My tears were not of regret for past transgressions or of anything prior to my bedroom encounter with the Holy Spirit a few weeks earlier. I wept because I could tangibly sense that, like the translucent people, the physical entrapment of my fleshly body was gone. It was as if my soul and spirit were finally free from the weight of the cares, disappointments, heartbreaks, addictions and chains of everything physically and mentally oppressive that this natural world heaps upon us. My very soul cried out with tears of joy that I was free and finally home.

As I lay there in a lake of cleansing tears, I looked up to see Jesus walking towards me. He came down off the stage and knelt beside me with His eyes full of love and His hands full of compassion. Then Jesus took His right hand and wiped the tears from my eyes. (Even now as I write this my eyes are refilling with tears as I sense the Holy Spirit taking me back to this moment. To Jesus, I give thanks and praise!)

Then, in that instant, a scroll was unveiled above the stage. It looked like a cloth banner unfolding in the wind behind an airplane (***Zechariah 5:2)***. On the scroll were these words, **"And God will wipe away every tear from their eyes."** Jesus then lifted me up and led me to the third part of this dream or vision.

(As a side note, I will add that months later I found the verse on that scroll. It is in ***Revelation 21:4***.)

Scripture references for Part Two:

> ***2 Corinthians 5:1-8** For we know that if our earthly house, this tent, is destroyed, we have a building from God, a house not made with hands, eternal in the heavens. ²For in this we groan, earnestly desiring to be clothed with our habitation which is*

from heaven, ³if indeed, having been clothed, we shall not be found naked. ⁴For we who are in this tent groan, being burdened, not because we want to be unclothed, but further clothed, that mortality may be swallowed up by life. ⁵Now He who has prepared us for this very thing is God, Who also has given us the Spirit as a guarantee. ⁶So we are always confident, knowing that while we are at home in the body we are absent from the Lord. ⁷For we walk by faith, not by sight. ⁸We are confident, yes, well pleased rather to be absent from the body and to be present with the Lord.

Matthew 25:31-46 ³¹"When the Son of Man comes in His glory, and all the holy angels with Him, then He will sit on the throne of His glory. ³²All the nations will be gathered before Him, and He will separate them one from another, as a shepherd divides his sheep from the goats. ³³And He will set the sheep on His right hand, but the goats on the left. ³⁴Then the King will say to those on His right hand, 'Come, you blessed of My Father, inherit the kingdom prepared for you from the foundation of the world, ³⁵for I was hungry and you gave Me food; I was thirsty and you gave Me drink; I was a stranger and you took Me in; ³⁶I was naked and you clothed Me; I was sick and you visited Me; I was in prison and you came to Me.' ³⁷"Then the righteous will answer Him, saying, 'Lord, when did we see You hungry and feed You, or thirsty and give You drink? ³⁸When did we see You a stranger and take You in, or naked and clothe You? ³⁹Or when did we see You sick, or in prison, and come to You?' ⁴⁰And the King will answer and say to them, 'Assuredly, I say to you, inasmuch as you did it to one of the least of these My brethren, you did it to Me.' ⁴¹"Then He will also say to those on the left hand, 'Depart from Me, cursed, into the everlasting fire prepared for the devil and his angels: ⁴²for I was hungry and you gave Me no food; I was thirsty and you gave Me no drink; ⁴³I was a stranger and you did not take Me in, naked and you did not clothe Me, sick and in prison and you did not visit Me.' ⁴⁴"Then they also will answer Him, saying, 'Lord, when did we see You hungry or thirsty or a stranger or naked or sick or in prison, and did not minister to You?' ⁴⁵Then He will answer them, saying, 'Assuredly, I say to you, inasmuch as you did not do it to one of the least of these, you did not do it to Me.' ⁴⁶And these will go away into everlasting punishment, but the righteous into eternal life."

John 16:5 – 15 ⁵"But now I go away to Him who sent Me, and none of you asks Me, 'Where are You going?' ⁶But because I have said these things to you, sorrow has filled your heart. ⁷Nevertheless I tell you the truth. It is to your advantage that I go away; for if I do not go away, the Helper will not come to you; but if I depart, I will send Him to you. ⁸And when He has come, He will convict the world of sin, and of righteousness, and of judgment: ⁹of sin, because they do not believe in Me; ¹⁰of righteousness, because I go to My Father and you see Me no more; ¹¹of judgment, because the ruler of this world is judged. ¹²"I still have many things to say to you, but you cannot bear them now. ¹³However, when He, the Spirit of truth, has come, He will guide you into all truth; for He will not speak on His own authority, but whatever He hears He will speak; and He will tell you things to come. ¹⁴He will glorify Me, for He will take of what is Mine and declare it to you. ¹⁵All things that the Father has are Mine. Therefore I said that He will take of Mine and declare it to you."

Revelation 1:17-18 ¹⁷And when I saw Him, I fell at His feet as dead. But He laid His right hand on me, saying to me, "Do not be afraid; I am the First and the Last. ¹⁸I am He who lives, and was dead, and behold, I am alive forevermore. Amen. And I have the keys of Hades and of Death.

Zechariah 5:2. And he said to me, "What do you see?" So I answered, "I see a flying scroll. Its length is twenty cubits and its width ten cubits."

Revelation 21:4. And God will wipe away every tear from their eyes; there shall be no more death, nor sorrow, nor crying. There shall be no more pain, for the former things have passed away."

The Flying Scroll

It has now been 34 years since I had the third heaven experience as detailed in the previous section called "The Stage Is Set." In that segment I saw the scroll flying through the air but never understood how God uses these "Flying Scrolls" or the deeper meaning of them. About a month ago when browsing through the Bible I saw the words "Flying Scroll" mentioned in ***Zechariah 5:2***.

Today I came across an article written 25 years ago which I found extremely interesting as it goes into more detail about the flying scroll. A short excerpt follows:

Biblical Horizons Newsletter
No. 67: A Flying Scroll
by Peter J. Leithart
November, 1994
Copyright 1994, Biblical Horizons

And he said to me, "What do you see?" And I answered, "I see a flying scroll; its length is twenty cubits and its width ten cubits." (Zechariah 5:2).

Immediately following his vision of the outpouring of the Spirit upon the restoration community (***Zech. 4:1-14***), Zechariah saw a flying scroll.

The scroll is mobile, not stationary.

A flying scroll is unusual enough, but this scroll is flying to and fro *unrolled*, or at least partly so. This is evident from the facts that Zechariah can estimate its dimensions (***Zech. 5:2***) and that he can see writing on both sides (***Zech. 5:3***). Scrolls normally roll into a tube as soon as you let go of the ends; evidently, someone has unrolled this scroll and is holding it open as it flies over the land. Breaking a scroll's seals and unrolling it signifies administering the things written in the scroll; as the Lamb unseals and unrolls the scroll, the words of the book become incarnate in history. (***Rev. 5:1ff***) The fact that the flying scroll is unrolled without *human* agency reinforces the message that the Lord Himself is unleashing the blessing contained therein.

Additional Scripture reference for the scroll:

> ***Revelation 5: 1-14.*** *And I saw in the right hand of Him who sat on the throne a scroll written inside and on the back, sealed with seven seals.* ***2*** *Then I saw a strong angel proclaiming with a loud voice, "Who is worthy to open the scroll and to loose its seals?"* ***3*** *And no one in heaven or on the earth or under the earth was able to open the scroll, or to look at it.* ***4*** *So I wept much, because no one was found worthy to open and read the scroll, or to look at it.* ***5*** *But one of the elders said to me, "Do not weep. Behold, the Lion of the tribe of Judah the Root of David, has prevailed to open the scroll and to loose its seven seals."* ***6*** *And I looked, and behold, in the midst of the throne and of the four living creatures, and in the midst of the elders, stood a Lamb as though it had been slain, having seven horns and seven eyes, which are the seven Spirits of God sent out into all the earth.* ***7*** *Then He came and took the scroll out of the right hand of Him who sat on the throne.* ***8*** *Now when He had taken the scroll, the four living creatures and the twenty-four elders fell down before the Lamb, each having a harp, and golden bowls full of incense, which are the prayers of the saints.* ***9*** *And they sang a*

new song, saying: "You are worthy to take the scroll, and to open its seals; for You were slain, and have redeemed us to God by Your blood Out of every tribe and tongue and people and nation, [10]And have made us kings and priests to our God; and we shall reign on the earth." [11]Then I looked, and I heard the voice of many angels around the throne, the living creatures, and the elders; and the number of them was ten thousand times ten thousand, and thousands of thousands, [12]saying with a loud voice: "Worthy is the Lamb who was slain to receive power and riches and wisdom, and strength and honor and glory and blessing!" [13]And every creature which is in heaven and on the earth and under the earth and such as are in the sea, and all that are in them, I heard saying: "Blessing and honor and glory and power be to Him who sits on the throne, And to the Lamb, forever and ever!" [14]Then the four living creatures said, "Amen!" And the twenty-four elders fell down and worshiped Him who lives forever and ever.

Part Three - The Offering

In this last segment of my dream, I was looking down into a great valley. Within the valley were multitudes of people of every race, creed, color, age and origin. Above this valley was a great brilliant light. I presumed in the dream that this brilliant light was a representation of God observing mankind below on the earth.

The people in the valley were trying to do anything and everything possible to get God's attention. They attempted to get noticed by making offerings to the "Holy and Almighty One" by helping a friend, singing religious songs, reading the Bible, dancing, reading intellectual or other highly recommended books, fasting, lamenting in prayer, giving money to the poor, tithing monies to their church and every other activity that could be perceived as a good work that may be noticed by God and, thus, having His favor imparted towards them. It was very clear that the motives of these people were to truly serve God. However, none of them in this place seemed able to get His attention or His sought-after approval.

Then I observed a small beam of light emanating from the brilliant light above the valley. It was shining below onto each of the people individually as if to examine their works. The light searched and searched, going from person to person, but **it did not find the perfect work for whch it was looking**.

You're Next

Once again, the Presence behind me placed His hand on my shoulder and drew me back towards Himself. He whispered in my ear, "Son, you're next."

In an instant I found myself on the valley floor amongst all the translucent people. Suddenly, the light, that had not found what it was looking for in the others, was shining upon me. It was like being an actor on a stage who has to perform for the audience even though the light is blinding them. Sensing the pressure to perform, I began feeling what the other people in the valley had been experiencing: feelings of anxiety, separation, hopelessness, bewilderment, confusion and frustration.

I thought to myself, "What can I possibly attempt to do to get God's approval that these people have not already tried?" The Presence behind me, that had never left me alone in this place, came to my rescue. With His hand once more upon my shoulder, He drew me back again towards Himself. With His voice close to my ear He whispered, "Son, sing this." I knew that my singing voice was about as good as a parrot squawking but obediently I began to sing what I heard and it went like this:

Jesus loves me, this I know,
For the Bible tells me so.
Little ones to Him belong.
They are weak, but He is strong.

Yes, Jesus loves me.
Yes, Jesus loves me.
Yes, Jesus loves me.
The Bible tells me so.

As I finished the song, the light surrounding me did not leave. It seemed the light of God had found the perfect offering that He had sought.

This part of the dream was to teach me that the perfection God seeks can **never** be found in our dogmatic good works according to:

> ***Ephesians 2:8-9. ⁸For by grace you have been saved <u>through faith</u>, and that not of yourselves; it is the gift of God, ⁹<u>not of works</u>, lest anyone should boast. (emphasis mine)***

Perfection is found only in the singular good work of Jesus Christ who died and shed His blood for our forgiveness; who was buried to defeat death's hold on our eternity; and rose again to be our Advocate with God the Father.

The song that I sang was a simple children's song that some of you may know. ***Jesus*** said in**:**

> ***Mark 10:13-16 ¹³Then they brought little children to Him, that He might touch them; but the disciples rebuked those who brought them. ¹⁴But when Jesus saw it, He was greatly displeased and said to them, "Let the little children come to Me, and do not forbid them; for of such is the kingdom of God. ¹⁵Assuredly, I say to you, whoever does not receive the kingdom of God <u>as a little child</u> will by no means enter it." ¹⁶And He took them up in His arms, laid His hands on them, and blessed them. (emphasis mine)***

Paul the apostle had kindred words like Jesus about how simple God has made it to attain eternal salvation. Paul wrote this:

> *2 Corinthians 11:3 But I fear, lest somehow, as the serpent deceived Eve by his craftiness, so your minds may be corrupted from the <u>simplicity</u> that is in Christ. (emphasis mine)*

This dream, along with hundreds of confirming Scriptures, has been a memorable resource as I have walked with the Lord Jesus Christ for the past 35 years and look forward to His promised return. In the days that followed this threefold dream, God created in me a hunger to read the Bible in its entirety.

To conclude this chapter, I would like to leave a few Scripture passages for you to ponder that show God's simplistic way to eternal salvation.

> *John 3:16-18 [16]For God so loved the world that He gave His only begotten Son, that whoever <u>believes in Him</u> should not perish but have everlasting life. [17]For God did not send His Son into the world to condemn the world, but that the world through Him might be saved. [18]He who believes in Him is not condemned; but he who does not believe is condemned already, because he has not believed in the name of the only begotten Son of God. (emphasis mine)*

> *Acts 4:12 Nor is there salvation in any other, for there is <u>no other name</u> under heaven given among men by which we must be saved. (emphasis mine)*

> *Romans 5:8 But God demonstrates His own love toward us, in that while we were still sinners, <u>Christ died</u> for us. (emphasis mine)*

> *Ephesians 1:7 <u>In Him</u> we have redemption through His blood, the forgiveness of sins, according to the riches of His grace. (emphasis mine)*

***John 1:12** But as many as <u>received Him</u>, to them He gave the right to become children of God, to those who believe in His name. (emphasis mine)*

***Romans 5:1** Therefore, having been justified <u>by faith</u>, we have peace with God through our Lord Jesus Christ. (emphasis mine)*

Chapter 3

So It Begins

As I said in chapters 1 and 2 it was in 1985 when I experienced the dreams and events that lead to my conversion to Christianity. At that time, I was working as a first line manager in a major food production facility. After my conversion, I have spent hundreds of hours studying biblical scripture. As a new believer, I just took the New Testament at face value and believed it as the "whole truth and nothing but the truth".

Grampa Rex on the Banana Peel

One day before leaving for work, I received a phone call from my mother telling me that Grampa Rex Addie was in the hospital and, if I wanted to see him one last time, I should go see him now. After that phone call I thought back to his life and how I had perceived him as I grew up.

Grampa Rex spent most of his life as a prison guard at Joliet State Penitentiary with some of the most hardened criminals in the state of Illinois. When I was growing up he would constantly degrade African Americans, Hispanics, and Asians as sub-human groups of people.

Being Caucasian, I had to overcome this false portrayal of those races, especially when I served in the United States Marine Corps. In the Corps, we all were the same color. As our drill instructors constantly reminded us, we were all GREEN and we all bled RED.

At that time one might say Grampa Rex was a very bigoted racist. He also was not very keen on going to church and only went to appease my Grandma Creta. Looking back now, I believe many people were praying for Grampa Rex's salvation since he did not display any signs of being a Christian.

After the phone call from my mother, I called into work to tell them I would not be there and began the drive to the hospital. I started thinking that, if Grampa Rex died, he would be subjected to Hell and the lake of fire for all eternity. I do not judge him here based on his works but solely on the basis that he had never received Jesus Christ's offer of forgiveness unto salvation that comes simply by accepting this gift of God that leads to eternal life.

Jesus tells us what convicts a person of eternal separation:

> *John 16:7-11 ⁷Nevertheless I tell you the truth. It is to your advantage that I go away; for if I do not go away, the Helper will not come to you; but if I depart, I will send Him to you. ⁸And when He has come, He will convict the world of sin, and of righteousness, and of judgment: ⁹of sin, <u>because they do not believe in Me;</u> ¹⁰of righteousness, because I go to My Father and you see Me no more; ¹¹of judgment, because the ruler of this world is judged. (emphasis mine)*

There is only one place I have ever found in the New Testament where the word *convict* is used with the Holy Spirit as a reference of doing the convicting and that is right here in verse 8. Notice also in verses 8 and 9 that the word "sin" is singular and not plural. The singular SIN that keeps anyone from eternal salvation is found in verse 9 which I have underlined. Jesus said "BECAUSE **THEY DO NOT BELIEVE IN ME**." PERIOD!

So, as I traveled that day, I began to ask God what part I could play, if any, in Him having mercy on Grampa Rex's life; that was, if his soul and spirit were not going to heaven. I got my answer when I arrived at the hospital.

Upon entering his room, I noticed that Grampa Rex was breathing in a very weird manner. I asked what his diagnosis was and was told that his heart was failing; he had cancer throughout his body; he had a blood virus that was expediting his departure; and he was Cheyne-Stoke breathing, which usually precedes death.

Cheyne–Stokes respiration (chān-stōks) is an **abnormal pattern of breathing** characterized by progressively deeper and sometimes faster breathing, followed by a gradual decrease that results in a temporary stop in breathing called an apnea. The pattern repeats, with each cycle usually taking 30 seconds to 2 minutes.

In other words, Grampa Rex had one foot in the grave and the other foot on a banana peel. In the room with me were his wife - my Grandmother Creta, his daughter - my Aunt Geane, and another person I will call Number Three.

As I stood there for a moment I could see a word picture of Scripture in my mind. (One of the gifts God has given me is the ability to recall Scripture at a moment's notice. This gift literally allows me to see a passage in my mind just as if I were holding an actual Bible in my hands.) Remember the verses in *John 16* we were just reviewing? Well, in the same passage Jesus speaks about this gift. He says:

> *John 16:13-15 [13]However, when He, the Spirit of truth, has come, He will guide you into all truth; for He will not speak on His own authority, but whatever He hears He will speak; and He will tell you things to come. [14]<u>He will glorify Me, for He will take of what is Mine and declare it to you.</u> [15]<u>All things that the Father has are Mine. Therefore, I said that He will take of Mine and declare it to you.</u> (emphasis mine)*

The verse I was being shown was:

> *Mark 16:15-18 [15]And He said to them, "Go into all the world and preach the gospel to every creature. [16]He who believes and is baptized will be saved; but he who does not believe will be condemned. [17]And these <u>signs</u> will follow those who believe: in*

my name they will cast out demons; they will speak with new tongues; ⁱ⁸ they will take up serpents; and if they drink anything deadly, it will by no means hurt them; <u>they will lay hands on the sick, and they will recover.</u>" (emphasis mine)

Yep, I told you I took the Bible literally as a new Christian and God had just directed me to "Lay hands on the sick, and they will recover." I may seem a little bolder in my writings after 35 years of walking with Jesus, but at that time I was not accustomed to praying for anyone in public, let alone praying a prayer for healing. However, if you are going to talk the talk, you had better be ready to walk the walk.

Seeming to speak boldly, I said to everyone in the room that I did not believe it was Grampa Rex's time to die. Inwardly I was freaking out that God would ask me to do this! This was a real faith builder indeed. I asked everyone in the room to gather around Grampa Rex's bed and hold hands while I prayed a ***Mark 16:18*** prayer for his complete healing.

Laying my hand on his forehead, I asked God the Father, in Jesus' name, to fulfill His promise in this verse if Grampa Rex was not ready to pass on for all eternity. I cursed the blood virus and cancer cells in Jesus' name and ordered his heart and lungs to be strengthened and healed in Jesus' name. It was a simple and to the point prayer. As I was leaving the room, they said they would call me if he passed that day. I smiled and walked out.

Three days passed before I received a phone call from Aunt Geane. She said that Grampa Rex had stopped the **Cheyne–Stokes respiration; his blood work showed the virus was <u>absent</u>; <u>no cancer</u> cells could be found; and his heart was functioning again at a <u>normal</u> level.**

She also mentioned that he was back home in his La-Z-Boy chair and, to my surprise, had picked up a Bible and was reading it! I guess the doctors were a little baffled at this point . . . . .

After I prayed that prayer, Grampa Rex lived about five more years and was in his 70s before he passed on. During that additional time, he gave his life to Jesus Christ and I know I will see him again one day. That experience was a benefit to *both* him and me. From that point forward I became more zealous and less intimidated about sharing God's love through Jesus Christ.

Barrenness to Blessing

While still employed at the food plant, I had a co-worker for whom I will use a fictitious name. Let's call him Mennis. Mennis was a practicing Catholic who was as open about his faith as I was with mine. Both of us were on third shift so we had a lot of time to talk without the corporate brass interrupting us.

Mennis and I were able to discuss in-depth why I did not have an earthly Catholic-type Father or priest to go to to confess my sins in order to receive forgiveness. I showed him in the Bible where Jesus Christ has now become our great High Priest and that we can now go directly through Jesus to the heavenly Father with all our prayer requests.

I shared my conversion dreams and the Grampa Rex story with him. He became very interested and indicated he was ready to test the waters of Christian faith. You see, Mennis and his wife could not have children. One or the other of them was barren and could not produce or receive what was needed to have children.

One day during one of our many biblical conversations, I showed Mennis the **Mark 16:18** verse about laying hands on the sick to be healed and also introduced him to this passage:

> *Matthew 18:18-19* [18] *"Assuredly, I say to you, whatever you bind on earth will be bound in heaven, and whatever you loose on earth will be loosed in heaven.* [19] *Again I say to you <u>that if two of you agree on earth concerning anything that they ask, it will be done for them by My Father in heaven</u>. (emphasis mine)*

I asked Mennis if he and his wife were serious about having children. He said they were. I told him that something might be sick in his body or hers so as not to be able to produce proper sperm counts or something else. So, I said, "Let's pray according to these two scriptures that, first, God will bring healing to the reproductive parts of your body or hers and, secondly, that we stand in agreement that God will fulfill His promise according to the words of Jesus Christ Himself confirming the prayer of agreement."

Without any Catholic priest there, I laid my hand on Mennis according to **Mark 16:18** and agreed with him according to **Matthew 18:19** that we were bound together in our prayer in Jesus' name for his wife and him to have children.

Well, long story short, within two months Mennis made a beeline to me to tell me that his wife was ***pregnant***. I was overjoyed for him and his wife that God was convincing this man to have a DIRECT relationship with our heavenly Father through Jesus Christ. No more priests for confessions for Mennis at this point as he began to go directly to God in Jesus' name on his own.

Now if one believes in God and His miracles, they should also believe there is a demonic realm that wants to destroy them or the good work God is doing in one's life. Shortly after the good news of Mennis' wife's pregnancy, I received word that Mennis had been in a serious car accident. Mennis had fallen asleep at the wheel on his way home from work. Yes, he was lucky, as it almost killed him.

When we had a chance to talk about it, I told him more about the demonic realm and how fallen angels want to destroy God's good things in our lives. Then I talked to him about the power of the Holy Spirit's protection. We again prayed together that he would be filled with the Holy Spirit and power according to **Acts chapter 1** and that God would protect him and his family.

Shortly after this Mennis and his wife invited me and another believer to their home where his wife gave her heart to Jesus as well. Mennis and his wife ended up having *eight* children by the time it was all said and done. All his children were raised in the Christian faith apart from Catholicism and all have become strong believers in Jesus.

As I finish this story about Mennis' spiritual victory, I am saddened to report that his wife no longer has her husband here on this earth. Mennis passed away from a heart attack a few years before I began writing this book. However, I am joyful that he has fulfilled his fatherly calling and is with Jesus now.

Demonic Resistance

During my time at this food production facility many heads were being turned at the change in me and other people like me. In this life one thing you can be sure of is this: if God is in the process of performing good works in someone, the demonic realm will attempt to ruin or thwart what God is doing. In my story about Mennis, I mentioned that he was nearly killed in an auto accident before he could enjoy the miracle of his first child's birth. This was interference by the demonic realm.

God's main goal for all humans on this earth is that they would come to believe in the good news or Gospel of His Son Jesus and that they may have eternal life with Him. Satan and the demonic realm know this and their primary goal is found in this verse:

1 Peter 5:8 Be sober, be vigilant; because your adversary the devil walks about like a roaring lion, <u>seeking whom he may devour</u>. (emphasis mine)

This almost happened to Mennis but as I was about to learn, there were others within my work group whose lives were at stake because they were being targeted by the demons in this evil realm. Most people think of the devil as Hollywood portrays him, as in some Amityville horror house flick or some other paranormal activity thriller. However, most of the time he will just use ordinary people who give in easily to the human fallen nature condition. The demonic realm uses fear, jealousy, envy, strife, selfish ambition, love of money, lust, greed, anger, power and so on to influence a negative outcome towards someone.

Please understand that once you begin to evangelize intensely, the demonic realm will be close behind your efforts working to **not** lose a soul to God. The demonic realm knows that it brings God no pleasure in seeing someone perish for eternity.

Ezekiel 33:11 Say to them: "As I live," says the Lord G*OD*, "I have no pleasure in the death of the wicked, but that the wicked turn from his way and live."

There were two people in my work group during those days that I believe fell prey to these dark forces. The demonic realm knew I was making great headway in turning people towards Jesus and an eternal life of happiness. First I will tell you about a person whom we will call Macie.

One Friday I went in to work and God placed Macie on my mind. I prayed for her throughout the day and asked God what I should be doing for Macie. Macie was supposed to go on a week's vacation and I really felt inside that something was terribly wrong.

Before the shift ended I took a moment and asked Macie what she had planned for her vacation. She really did not say so we just made small talk until I just had to ask her point blank. I said, "Macie, for some reason the good Lord put you on my mind today." She said that she was a Baptist and everything was going to be just fine. She left work at the end of her shift and off on vacation she went.

That following Monday I received notice that a funeral service for Macie would be later that week. I was asked to notify all of her friends at Frito Lay that they were invited to the wake and funeral. You see, friend, Macie did not die of natural causes. The weekend after she left for vacation someone put three .38 caliber slugs in her chest. Yes, the person who did it was probably drunk or was mentally influenced to kill her by something in the demonic realm.

The second person I want to tell you about is a woman we will call Banet. Like Macie, Banet was scheduled to go on vacation for two weeks. God put her on my mind as well and, like with Macie, I inquired about her plans for her vacation. Banet said they were taking an RV through the Colorado mountains and planned to stay at different campsites along the way. As I had done with Macie, I told Banet that the good Lord had put her on my mind and I asked her to be careful. When I mentioned "good Lord" her face changed. Giving me a stone-cold glare she walked away without another word.

Well, about a week later, I got notification of her wake and funeral as well. It appeared that "something" made their RV go over the side of a mountain in Colorado. Everyone inside was killed. I look back on those events and it was almost like the movie called "Final Destination." I can only hope that Banet and her husband had received salvation sometime before their untimely deaths.

Demonic Harassment

Remember in our last segment that I told you the demonic realm will use other people to try to stop you from being effective in your quest for evangelism? I showed you in real time stories how Satan went after the people who worked for me.

The demonic realm cannot stop you from sharing Jesus with other people because **the Holy Spirit resides *in* you.** They will try to intimidate you into compliance by using other humans in higher authority over you.

In my case, I had, in my opinion, an alcoholic boss who was a mean drunk. He would come in during the late night third shift and harass me and my employees. If he was not doing that, he would just sit and sleep in a bathroom stall for half the night and then stumble around the place until the next shift started. By that time he would be sober enough to give his shift report to the plant production manager.

He found me less tolerable after my conversion to faith in Jesus as I must have represented something that he was missing in his life.

He made sure to frequently inform the plant production manager that my religion was getting in the way of my job.

In reality, he would create chaos during the shift and force major production equipment to be shut down. At times this would create less than average production rates because of his drunken decisions over which I had no control. In his reports he made sure that I was the one thrown under the bus for low production. To the employees and most other managers, including his 2nd line peers, his behavior was a well-known joke throughout the plant.

One day the plant production manager called me into his office and asked me why, at various times, we had lower production numbers (as if he really didn't know). We will call this guy Pott for this story's purposes. He went on to say that he was told that I talk too much about my religion with other employees and that may be why the numbers were lower.

Another time, he took his ball point pen out of his pocket and held it up to me. He said, "If I don't see some of the production numbers change, I am going to have to raise this pen against you and you know what that means." Now at this point I should have been intimidated by his eloquent little speech; however, the moment he said those threatening words to me, the Holy Spirit put a word picture story instantly into my mind. God said that this is what the Holy Spirit will do for you when harassed and put into these kinds of positions:

> *Luke 12:11-12 Jesus said: [11] "Now when they bring you to the synagogues and magistrates and authorities, do not worry about how or what you should answer, or what you should say. [1] For the Holy Spirit will teach you in that very hour what you ought to say."*

So instead of throwing my boss under the bus, I looked deeply into his eyes and said, "Pott, I have a story for you." Then I told him this parable.

"Once there was a man who had a dog. This dog was a faithful dog and always looked for ways to please his master. Every day this dog would go out and retrieve the newspaper for his master. It did not matter if it was raining, storming, freezing, scorching hot, or hailing. The master's dog would wait hours for the paper to arrive and guard it against any other thieving dogs that would try to steal it once it was delivered.

"After the dog got the newspaper he would bring it into the house to where the master sat and lay it at his feet. The master would take the paper and read about what was going on in the world around him. For years this dog was diligent to repeat the process. In all those years of faithfulness and diligent service, the master never gave the dog a 'good boy!' or any other kind of positive affirmation.

"After a while the master became enraged at what the paper said because the world around him was changing. So, after he read the newspaper, he would roll the paper up and throw it in the faithful and diligent dog's face. The dog was surprised at his master's response.

"Had he not been faithful and diligent all these years to bring the master his newspaper every day? The dog thought, 'I have so little say in what is printed in the paper, yet my master blames me for his world's problems.' Yet through all this the dog remained faithful and diligent.

"The master began to drink alcohol heavily every day prior to receiving his paper. When the dog promptly brought him the paper, the master would rip it out of his mouth. After reading it, the master would become enraged about what the paper said. Instead of throwing it in the dog's face, he started rolling up the paper and began beating the dog with it."

Pausing, I looked deeply into Pott's eyes and said, "After a while, what do you think that dog is going to do for the master?" After I said this, Pott's face was as white as a ghost and he looked like he had seen one as well.

Pott got up out of his chair and walked away muttering something about needing an attitude change. I am not sure what nerve I touched or what secret issues the Holy Spirit made click in his mind, but, from then on, Pott avoided me like the plague at manager meetings, would not look me in the eye and avoided occupying any space within 20 feet of me. I know the Holy Spirit revealed something to Pott from the story I told him that only Pott and God knew about. This story is but one of the many times God would give me a word picture story at a moment's notice in the years to come.

If there is one solid thing I can say about God's Holy Spirit, it is that one cannot best Him in a match of wits, wisdom, debate, knowledge, insight or history.

When man and his wisdom come against you, you will be utterly amazed at what comes out of your mouth when the Holy Spirit is in you or comes upon you. Some Scriptures to support this are:

> ***Matthew 10:19-20** [19]But when they deliver you up, take no thought how or what you should speak: for it will be given to you in that hour what you should speak. [20]For it is not you who speak, but the Spirit of your Father who speaks in you.*

> ***Romans 8:31-32** [31]What shall we then say to these things? If God be for us, who can be against us [32]He that spared not His own Son, but delivered Him up for us all, how shall He not with Him also freely give us all things?*

Nothing ever came from that meeting, but I am sure Pott will never forget that time nor the story that I told. I think most of you reading this get the analytical meaning behind this simple story. Scripture says in:

> ***Proverbs 3:5-6** [5]Trust in the Lord with all your heart, and lean not on your own understanding; [6]in all your ways acknowledge Him, and He shall direct your paths. (emphasis mine)*

Moving on

In the late 1980s, the food plant where I was working had a mass layoff of hundreds of first line managers. Unfortunately, I fell into their layoff mix. Fortunately, I had made enough income that I could draw a good chunk of unemployment change until I could transition into my next phase of employment.

When things like this happen in our work world we can worry, panic, stagnate or ride the free lunch train until the track ends and then settle for less. <u>My personal belief as a believer in Jesus Christ is that He is a **promoter** of His children's work world and not a **demoter**</u>.

It is at times like this, when your faith and His goodness towards us shines throughout our darkest times or our deepest fears. We can listen to what the news, family, friends, or economic forecast is, or we can stand on what God has said in the Bible about the matter. One of my favorite passages is:

> ***Ephesians 3:20-21*** *[20]Now to Him <u>who is able to do exceedingly abundantly above all that we ask or think</u>, according to the power that works in us, [21]to Him be glory in the church by Christ Jesus to all generations, forever and ever. Amen. (emphasis mine)*

A short time after this I began a business in the water cooler and snack food vending field. Basically, I went into a small business that used bottle-less water coolers. I showed businesses how to get rid of all those pesky five-gallon bottles at a fraction of the cost. Once in the business I was usually able to set them up on a snack food vending service as well.

My heart's design for the business was not so much the monetary gains, but the inroads it gave me to share the Gospel of Jesus Christ with people on a one to one basis. The business grew fairly quickly till over 500 accounts were realized. I enjoyed my time getting to know my clients on a personal level and being more like a pastor to them than a water and snack food provider.

A Time of Review

It had been about three years since my conversion and my time ending at the food processing plant. I have never regretted any negative fallout for choosing to follow the Christian path of faith and salvation in Jesus Christ alone.

I look back at all the works the Holy Spirit did during those times and I realize there was a pattern as to why they occurred. It was during this time of my life when starting my new business that I had the privilege of spending a couple years as a volunteer at a homeless shelter in Beloit, Wisconsin. Every third Sunday, I was tasked with giving the morning sermon or message to the church that also assembled there.

It was through this ministry that I did my due diligence and received my written ordination as a minister of the Gospel of Jesus Christ.

Chapter 4

Breanna

This chapter is dedicated to my daughter Breanna. This beautiful human being has been a Godly instrument in teaching me insights from God. You who are parents can fully appreciate the trials, testings, sacrifices and lessons that our children bring into our lives. However, as the days go by, we can better understand how God Himself has chosen to call us His children by the actions we see from our own limited experiences. Here are a couple of memories and God lessons I learned from Breanna at a tender age. But first, here is a quote from BibleGodQuotes.com:

> *"Only God can*
> *Turn a mess into a message,*
> *A test into a testimony,*
> *A trial into a triumph,*
> *A victim into a victory."*

The Sacrifice

It was well into the running of my own business that I married. From this union was born my blessed daughter, Breanna. What a beautiful gift from God she was and is! She stole my heart at her birth. When she was very young this blonde, curly haired and blue-eyed miracle from God became a test of my faith and a "Miracle" for me.

At 17 months old my daughter was "Failing to Thrive," as the medical term so aptly states. She stopped gaining weight and had begun losing what remaining weight she had. When she dropped down to 17 pounds and became very dehydrated, she was hospitalized.

I clearly remember sitting next to her hospital bed and looking at her little arm strapped to a board with an IV sticking out of her arm through which she received her nutrition. Her big blue eyes stared at me with the assurance that she was going to be OK because her Father was there with her.

However, a father needs a Father to console him when it comes to the deep matters of the heart. You see, my heart loved this child and I would have gladly traded places with her.

As I prayed to my Heavenly Father about her, a series of thoughts were presented to my mind. In hindsight, I believe that God was the One that had introduced the following considerations:

First, I knew that God can see the future of one's existence and knows the decisions that a person is going to make along the way.

Second, knowing this, I wondered if God knew that my daughter was *not* going to accept Jesus Christ as her Savior and would be eternally damned.

Thirdly, if that was the case, would I as her earthly Father, ask God the Heavenly Father to take her now to Heaven knowing that one day I would see her again in eternity? Or would I be selfish and scripturally demand that God heal her and roll the dice that I would by my own power guide her into a future salvation experience with Jesus?

Oh, yes, before I go too far, here is a verse concerning children's salvation based on a parent's belief before an age of accountability:

1 Corinthians 7:14** **For the unbelieving husband is sanctified by the wife, and the unbelieving wife is sanctified by the husband;

otherwise your children would be unclean, but now they are holy.

As I pondered these thoughts, my mind went back to Abraham in the Old Testament who was instructed by God to sacrifice his son Isaac on an altar to God (***Genesis 22***). Abraham did as he was told but God stopped Abraham right at the point of carrying it through. Abraham was tested that day to give up the very son he loved and he passed the test.

The reality of Abraham's story that God was demonstrating hundreds of years BC was that He was going to send His "ONLY BEGOTTEN SON – Jesus Christ", the Son whom He loved, and would willingly lay Him on the sacrificial altar where He would be killed by His own creation, that is mankind, so that He might save mankind by that very blood sacrifice for the atonement of all our sin.

The bottom line in my test was this: was I going to trust God's will for my daughter, be it passing into eternity or remaining here to fulfill a divine purpose one day?

Well, I took the path of Abraham and asked God that His will be done. Yes, I believe God was testing my heart that day. I figured that if "God is Love," then His ultimate decision would be out of love for my daughter's eternal destiny and not <u>my</u> momentary gratification. It was a day or two later that the doctors discovered my daughter might possibly have celiac disease.

So, what is celiac disease?

Celiac disease (also known as celiac sprue or gluten intolerance) is a digestive disorder that damages the small intestine. This damage interferes with the absorption of nutrients from food. People with celiac disease cannot tolerate **gluten**, *a protein found mainly in wheat, rye and barley. It's also found in everyday products such as medicines, vitamins and lip balms.*

When a person with celiac disease eats gluten, the immune system responds by attacking the lining of the small intestine and destroying villi – tiny finger-like protrusions lining the small intestine. Villi allow nutrients from food to be absorbed through the walls of the intestine and into the bloodstream.

Well, I had my answer. God not only tested my heart that day to see if I would trust Him, but He also gave her back to me with a diagnosis that could save her life. Once we stopped feeding her foods that contained gluten, she began to thrive and gain weight again.

This discovery was a real miracle as at this time the medical community knew very little about celiac disease. I thank God for giving a doctor the wisdom to have her intestinal lining tested at a cutting edge lab leading to making this discovery. Through this experience He also confirmed to me that she would become a believer in the Gospel of Jesus Christ and I would have an eternity with her.

That was 24 years ago. My daughter has now become a healthy young woman on a path with a personal relationship of her own with God. Praise His name forever!

The Sting

Moving on. I named this section "The Sting" because of another situation that my beloved daughter went through.

It was a sunny day and my daughter was out in front of the house playing with some neighbor kids on the sidewalk. She was wearing a colorful light-colored play dress. I was in the house when I suddenly heard a bloodcurdling scream coming from the front yard.

I ran outside to see my daughter swatting at herself as if trying to get something off of her. By the time I reached her I noticed several German hornets flying around her seemingly attracted to the colors of her dress.

By this time she was crying hysterically. She lifted her arm and showed me three big welts from the stings the German hornets had inflicted on her. I brought her in the house and her mother cared for the wounds.

As a former United States Marine Corps veteran, I took this attack upon my daughter in a deeply personal way. To me it was time for *every* German hornet on the face of the planet to DIE.

So, in fine tradition of the Marine Corps, I set my mind to methodically figuring out a way to KILL EVERY ONE OF THESE LITTLE DEMONS FROM HELL. I did my research and rigged up a hornet trap that I purchased at a local big box store. The trap was unique in that it was designed to lure, trap and then *slowly* kill. "A fitting end," I thought, for these little beasts.

The trap was to be filled with soda pop as the lure. I used Mountain Dew as it had the most sugar and visual drawing power, kind of like leaving an open can of soda on a picnic bench and finding it full of hornets before you could take your next drink.

You then were to add liquid dish soap to the soda inside the trap. The trap was made so it was easy for the hornets to crawl inside. Once they did, it was all but impossible to escape while their wings were extended in flight. They would get tired and fall into the Mountain Dew/dish soap mixture. The dish soap would get on their wings and make them heavy. So, no matter how many times they tried to escape by flight, they would simply keep falling back into the Mountain Dew mixture until they drowned.

To my delight this trap worked per its design. It worked so well that I went out and bought several more and put them all over the yard. That first year I killed literally thousands of those little child molesters.

Now, unbeknownst to me, God was going to use Breanna's little tragedy for His own purpose. Early one weekend morning I was pulling weeds from around the hosta plants along the cement walkway that led up to our front door. As I did, I noticed a German hornet buzz past me weighed down with pollen from its trip around the neighborhood. Sure enough, the greedy little thing just had to get the Mountain Dew in my trap. I watched it go in, do the escape dance and then drown in a green sea with his fellow kin that had come in before him.

As I went back to my weed pulling task, I heard a voice say something to the effect of, "Hello, we are in your neighborhood today talking to people about the Bible."

Standing there on my walkway was a young couple whom I recognized by their garb as a pair of Jehovah's Witnesses.

Now Wikipedia describes this *cult* as follows:

> ***Jehovah's Witnesses*** *is a <u>millenarian</u> <u>restorationist</u> <u>Christian denomination</u> <u>with</u> <u>nontrinitarian</u> <u>beliefs</u> <u>distinct</u> <u>from</u> **<u>mainstream Christianity</u>**.*

Now, that is quite a mouthful of big descriptive words that basically mean they do not believe in the Trinity, the Father, the Son, and the Holy Ghost as Christians believe. Jehovah's Witnesses believe salvation is obtained by a combination of faith, good works, and obedience. This contradicts countless Scriptures which declare salvation to be received **by grace through faith** (**John 3:16, Ephesians 2:8-9, Titus 3:5**). Jehovah's Witnesses reject the Trinity, believing Jesus to be a created being and the Holy Spirit to essentially be the inanimate power of God.

Most importantly, Jesus HIMSELF spoke of the Holy Trinity when giving the Great Commission:

> *Matthew 18:18-20* [18]*And Jesus came and spoke to them (the eleven disciples), saying "All authority has been given to Me in heaven and on earth.* [19]*Go therefore and make disciples of all nations, baptizing them in the name of <u>the Father</u>, and of <u>the Son</u>, and of <u>the Holy Spirit</u>,* [20]*teaching them to observe all*

things that I have commanded you; and lo, I am with you always, even to the end of the age." Amen. (emphasis mine)

Anyway, there they were, all ready to have a great debate about biblical theology on my front sidewalk. As I stood up to talk with them, an idea from God popped into my head like a picture pasted on a billboard.

"Quick, follow me," I said. "You have got to see this." They both looked at me, baffled that I was not giving them the traditional sidewalk discussion for which they were groomed. I had them follow me about thirty feet to where my hornet traps were. I said to them, "Now watch this." As we all stared at the trap a German hornet came along, made his way into the trap, did the dance, fell over and drowned in the body-laden cesspool of old hornet carcasses.

Then I turned to them and looking squarely into their eyes. I said, "Did you just see what happened here?" I continued, "That German hornet has been all over this neighborhood trying to do what his hornet DNA wanted of him. Before he went into this trap, his legs were already loaded down with pollen. I am sure that was a heavy burden for that poor little guy. Yet, despite his heavy burden, he continued until he was finally trapped and his heavy cargo only hastened his demise, making him sink to the bottom where he drowned."

Then I said, "First of all, I know you are with the Jehovah's Witnesses. I am very familiar with your theology. I do not agree with it, but I do wish the Christian community would have the same zeal and compassion that you two have to be able to get out and share your faith. Secondly, you two and your sect are much like this German hornet, canvassing a neighborhood thinking that you are doing the right thing for your colony.

"Yet, the more canvassing that you do, the more you will begin to question what you believe which will begin to weigh down your soul, just like that German hornet, as you begin to question the validity of what you believe. Eventually, like the German hornet, you will feel trapped inside the questionable theology of others and you will either leave the sect, turn to another form of religion, or just quit religion altogether."

The young man quickly grabbed his Bible and turned to:

> ***James 2: 19-20** **19** You believe that there is one God. You do well. Even the demons believe — and tremble! **20** But do you want to know, O foolish man, that faith without works is dead?*

He quoted me the passage to play down my German hornet story, basically telling me that God demands that we work, like the German hornet did, for our salvation.

I smiled and said, "I don't have a Bible on me but you can turn to:

> ***Ephesians 2:8-9** **8** For by grace you have been saved through faith, and that not of yourselves; it is the gift of God, **9** <u>not of works</u>, lest anyone should boast."*

Before he could respond, I went on, "I know that your Universal Edition of the Bible blots out the text agreed upon by most scholars but I want to leave you with this. Most people in my Christian faith will never go read verse **10** of that same passage. That passage finishes by stating:

> ***Ephesians 2:10** For we are His workmanship, created in Christ Jesus for good works, which God prepared <u>beforehand</u> that we should walk in them."*

I asked, "Did you get that? In Jesus Christ, I was created for good works and those good works were prepared beforehand until the day God wants me to bring them to fruition." I smiled. "Today you are standing here in front of me because God chose *this* day for me to do a good work.

"He knew you were coming and set up the whole German hornet story just for you two. God wants you to know that one day you will grow weary of trying to work your way into His good graces to possibly be one of his 144,000 chosen ones.

"When that day comes, and it will, God wants you to know that you can be *instantly* saved and in His eternal graces by believing that this Jesus is God, a part of the Trinity, that He died on a cross for your unbelief concerning Him, and rose again to give you eternal life."

Finishing, I quoted:

Romans 10:13 For whosoever shall call upon the name of the Lord will be saved. (KJV)

"Remember this day, my young friends, and ask God to give you eternal life through Jesus Christ His Son. You see, if I choose never to tell another person about Jesus Christ in my life, I will *still* go to Heaven. This is based on what Jesus Christ did according to the Gospel and not what I ever do for Him in my life."

With that I turned away and left two very shocked and stunned JW evangelists to ponder my words. I noticed that in the following days and years, as long as I lived on that street, all future JW's passed right on by my house like we had the plague. I am sure though that these two JW followers will never forget the German hornet story for the rest of their lives for God has put millions of German hornets in His creation to remind them of this day every time one tries to get inside their can of soda pop. I pray that by now one or both has turned to Jesus Christ and are living a life free of a "works righteousness" based cult faith.

A New Creation

While driving home one day, Breanna and I passed by a large cemetery full of headstones and statues. As we continued to drive past this place every day, Breanna became inquisitive and asked me what that place was with all the flowers and statues. Off the cuff and without any thought, I told her that this place was called a graveyard. I went on to say that when people die, they are buried there so their families can visit and remember them.

Later that evening, I was getting ready to tuck Breanna into bed. She was nearing five years old at this time. As was our custom, we knelt down beside her bed to say our bedtime prayers. As her blue eyes met mine, a troubled look crossed her face.

In a tearful voice, she said, "Daddy, promise me that if I die, you will not throw me in a cold hole and cover me with dirt." My mind instantly pictured my sweet little girl six feet down, struggling for air and calling for her Daddy to come help her. The utter helplessness she must have been feeling filled my soul. I was sure that a shocked, stunned and horrified look was on my face.

However, our God is faithful and gives us wisdom. I was reminded of what Jesus said the Holy Spirit would do for us at a moment like this in:

> *John 16:5-15* *⁵"But now I go away to Him who sent Me, and none of you asks Me, 'Where are You going?' ⁶But because I have said these things to you, sorrow has filled your heart. ⁷Nevertheless I tell you the truth. <u>It is to your advantage that I go away; for if I do not go away, the Helper will not come to you; but if I depart, I will send Him to you.</u> ⁸And when He has come, He will convict the world of sin, and of righteousness, and of judgment: ⁹of sin, because they do not believe in Me; ¹⁰of righteousness, because I go to My Father and you see Me no more; ¹¹of judgment, because the ruler of this world is judged.¹² "I still have many things to say to you, but you cannot bear them now. ¹³<u>However, when He, the Spirit of Truth, has come, He will guide you into all truth; for He will not speak on His own authority, but whatever He hears He will speak; and He will tell you things to come.</u> ¹⁴He will glorify Me, for He will*

<u>take of what is Mine and declare it to you.</u> ¹⁵All things that the Father has are Mine. Therefore, I said that He will take of Mine and declare it to you." (emphasis mine)

As suddenly as her fearful thought was thrust upon me a word picture story was birthed in my mind. I mean, in an instant, I could see the whole story that I needed to pass on to her. So, allowing the Holy Spirit to take control of the conversation, I asked Breanna this question. "Do you know what a seed is?" She replied, "Yes, Daddy, you put it in the ground." "That's right," I said. "You dig a little hole in the ground and put the seed in it."

Then I asked, "What do you do next, Breanna?" At this question, she gave me that 'Do you think I am stupid or what?' look. LOL She replied, "Well, you cover it up with dirt, of course." "That's right, Honey," I said. Then I asked, "What do you think happens *after* you cover up the seed with dirt?" She replied, "I think it grows, Daddy." "That's right," I affirmed. "After you cover up a seed with dirt, the sun's light begins to warm up the seed, and, given enough time, the seed becomes alive again. When it does, it comes out of the ground as a beautiful new creation."

I took her little hand in mine and asked, "Breanna, do you remember the pictures we have shown you that were taken when you were just a little baby?" "Oh, yes, Daddy. I was *little* then." I chuckled a tad because she was still my *little* baby. "Well," I continued, "Now you are not a little baby anymore, are you?" She was quick to agree and stated that she was a *big girl* now which brought another chuckle from me.

"Very soon you will be older like your big brother, go to school and make friends," I said. "Then as time goes on you will become older like Mommy and Daddy are now." She replied, "That's not very old at all, Daddy." I jokingly thought to myself, 'Bless you, my child' as I no longer felt like an eighteen-year-old basketball star or a strapping young United States Marine.

Continuing I said, "Then after a long time we all grow up to be like your Grandpa and Grandma." She answered, "That's OLD, Daddy." Then I asked, "Do you remember the little seed we plant in the ground?" "Yes, Daddy," she replied. "After you get older like Grandma and Grandpa, you have one last thing to do." "What's that?" she asked. "Well," I answered, "We go through a natural process called death and we die. After we die, we become just like that seed."

"Breanna," I asked, "Do you know what a peanut looks like?" She said, "Yes, Daddy, it has a hard part on the outside but a little peanut on the inside." "Well," I replied, "When we die, our hard shell that looks like Grandma and Grandpa needs to be buried. So, our friends will dig a little hole and put that old shell in it and cover it up with dirt."

Then I added, "Remember the little peanut inside that old shell? Well, that part of us doesn't get buried. The little peanut is who we really are on the inside. Jesus has promised to take the best part of us to Heaven while we wait for our old shell to grow.

"Remember, God has promised us that when our old shell is buried, He will let His Son's light shine on that old shell because we believe that Jesus will bring us back to life again. When Jesus comes back some day, His light will cause all of us who believe in Him to come out of the ground as beautiful new people who will live forever with Jesus."

Then Breanna said, "Daddy, I already asked Jesus to be my Savior. So that means I will come back as a big beautiful new person, right?" I answered, "Breanna, you are so smart and you are right. Not only you, but your Mommy and I will be beautiful new people as well. We will all live together with Jesus forever."

With a smile on her face she asserted, "I bet Jesus has a lot of little peanuts in Heaven with Him right now." "Indeed He does, Breanna," I affirmed. "They are all waiting for Jesus to come back and make them beautiful new people again, but until that day, they are safe with Him."

Then with a giggle, a kiss and a long hug, my beautiful little daughter crawled into bed and rested her head peacefully on her pillow and fell asleep like the baby I knew she still was.

God's Humor

My daughter, Breanna, and I have continued to have many more encounters learning together about God's ever presence in our daily lives which has helped us grow closer together. I would like to share a quick story about how humorous our Heavenly Father can be.

One day when Breanna was about ten years old, she was walking out of a grocery store with me. It was drizzling rain and Breanna ran ahead to the car so she would not get wet. To me this was just a minor dripping compared to some of the weather conditions I had lived through while in the Marine Corps.

So, while she was opening the car doors, I went into Marine Corps mental mode and told her to tough it out. I stopped walking right behind the car just to show her how to ride out a little rain.

Once I saw that she had noticed that I was just standing there, I pulled a bad boy Dad act for her. I stretched out my hands, looked up into the sky and asked, "God, is that all You've got?" I had barely gotten the words out of my mouth when the skies opened up like Noah's flood and instantly a torrential rain poured onto my face and drenched my entire body.

Then I heard Breanna laughing hysterically as she said, "Well, you did ask God if that was all He had." I am almost sure I heard laughter from Heaven rippling through the raindrops as God had some fun not only humbling me but, most of all, showing Breanna that He is ever present and lighthearted in His nature.

Gregory Addie

Chapter 5

God's Representative "The Ambassador"

2 Corinthians 5: 14-20 *¹⁴For the love of Christ compels us, because we judge thus: that if One died for all, then all died; ¹⁵and He died for all, that those who live should live no longer for themselves, but for Him who died for them and rose again. ¹⁶Therefore, from now on, we regard no one according to the flesh. Even though we have known Christ according to the flesh, yet now we know Him thus no longer. ¹⁷Therefore, if anyone is in Christ, he is a new creation; old things have passed away; behold, all things have become new. ¹⁸Now all things are of God, who has reconciled us to Himself through Jesus Christ, and has given us the ministry of reconciliation, ¹⁹that is, that God was in Christ reconciling the world to Himself, not imputing their trespasses to them, and has committed to us the word of reconciliation. ²⁰Now then, <u>we are ambassadors for Christ</u>, as though God were pleading through us: we implore you on Christ's behalf, be reconciled to God. (emphasis mine)*

In this chapter, I would like to revisit some of the many "Holy Spirit-planned" experiences that I have walked into through my lifetime. My hope for you readers, who are still on the fence concerning salvation through Jesus Christ, is that in reading my non-fiction real life testimonies, you will find some convincing and compelling evidence to believe in Christ.

By telling you how I became a believer in this Jesus, I have brought you to this point but I have yet to demonstrate His real time power that can be in *your* lives.

Definitions of an ambassador are listed below. These three definitions are taken from secular and original biblical Greek text definitions. They are as follows:

Am·bas·sa·dor *[am'basədər] an accredited diplomat sent by a country as its official representative to a foreign country: (synonyms: envoy, plenipotentiary, emissary,·(papal) nuncio, representative, high commissioner, consul, consul general, diplomat, legate) a person who acts as a representative or promoter of a specified activity: "he is a good ambassador for the industry" synonyms: campaigner,· representative·, promoter·, champion·, supporter,· backer·, booster*

Ambassador *(from Wikipedia)*: *An ambassador is the ranking government representative stationed in a foreign* capital. *The host country typically allows the ambassador control of specific territory called an* embassy, *whose territory, staff, and vehicles are generally afforded* diplomatic immunity *in the host country. Under the* Vienna Convention on Diplomatic Relations, *an ambassador has the highest* diplomatic rank.

Walking Out the Ambassador Calling

Throughout the later chapters of this book are real time examples of some of the work the Holy Spirit has accomplished during my life thus far. I say the Holy Spirit because it is truly because of **His** leading, guiding, prompting, understanding, mercy and compassion that you or I, or any of us who actively engage in acting out this ambassador's role, can accomplish anything. One only needs to read the biblical book of *Acts* to see that this is true. I really think the writer(s) of *Acts* should have entitled it "The Acts of THE HOLY SPIRIT."

Let's revisit some of these "Acts of the Holy Spirit."

Crusade for Christ

Back in my junior year in high school, I had a friend named John. John was a Catholic guy that never shared his faith much, but he loved music.

At that time the local protestant churches would get together once a year and have a "Crusade for Christ" at our local fairgrounds. This was in the early 1970s when churches actually took the Great Commission seriously and came together as one county church with the sole purpose of growing its membership. Their members invited non-believing friends, family and acquaintances for music and a Gospel message.

As a side note, I will mention that this was discontinued by the 1980s as local churches began to segregate themselves based on theological differences. What most churches have failed to realize over the past four decades is that a thriving church is like a living lake of water. A lake that stays clean and supports aquatic life has fresh water coming into it and water outflow leaving it on a continual basis.

This exchange of waters creates oxygen for the lake to thrive. If the fresh water were cut off, the lake would stagnate and die. In this analogy, that means fresh converts to Jesus in the front door and refined teachers, preachers, evangelists, apostles, pastors and core believers out the back door to fulfill various callings and propagate the Gospel of Jesus Christ via the GREAT COMMISSION.

Anyway, knowing John liked music, I invited him to one of the local Crusades. My inviting him was a miracle in itself as my lifestyle at the time was very secular in nature. Yes, God's Spirit can use any one of us to lead another to Jesus even when your current lifestyle is scripturally off balance. A traveling family group called the Lundstroms provided the music and speaker. I watched John begin to stare as the group played song after song about Jesus. Then Lowell Lundstrom gave a salvation message and an altar call for everyone who wanted to accept Jesus as their Savior to come to the front for prayer.

To my utter shock and amazement, John got up and walked down to the front to become a believer in Jesus Christ! I share this story with you because of the way it ends. **You see, one year later John was walking down a road at dusk and was hit from behind by a car. John died instantly that night. He is now with Jesus for eternity because of his decision that one night to believe in Jesus Christ.**

Through the years I have learned to listen very carefully when the Holy Spirit puts a thought in my mind. Now you may ask, "How do you know it is the Holy Spirit speaking to you?"

For me, it is when His <u>presence accompanies the thought</u>. His presence you may ask? Think of a worship service that you may have been in during your life. Remember that <u>peaceful</u>, cleansing, goose bump feeling? Here is a verse worth meditating:

> *Philippians 4:6-7 ⁶Be anxious for nothing, but in everything by prayer and supplication, with thanksgiving, let your requests be made known to God; ⁷and the <u>peace of God, which surpasses all understanding</u>, will guard your hearts and minds through Christ Jesus. (emphasis mine)*

Now, on the other hand, if the thought is not of the Holy Spirit, I will literally feel like I am getting kicked from the inside out down in my gut. I call that a GUT CHECK.

Here are several supporting Scripture verses to validate this kind of inner communication:

> *John 14:17 The Spirit of Truth, whom the world cannot receive, because it neither sees Him nor knows Him; but you know Him, for He dwells with you and will be in you.*

***Romans 8:11** But if the Spirit of Him who raised Jesus from the dead dwells in you, He who raised Christ from the dead will also give life to your mortal bodies through His Spirit who dwells in you.*

***1 Corinthians 3:16** Do you not know that you are the temple of God and that the Spirit of God dwells in you?*

A DOG NAMED REX

OK, let's continue down the path of how the Holy Spirit communicates with us. Over the years I have been asked on occasion to be a guest speaker at various functions. I remember being invited to share a message at a men's breakfast to be held before their usual church service.

Coming up with the right message can be difficult at times, if not downright torturing mentally. After much struggling, I felt led to talk about self-righteousness from this passage which says*:*

***Philippians 3:1-14** Finally, my brethren, rejoice in the Lord. To write the same things to you, to me indeed is not grievous, but for you it is safe ²Beware of dogs, beware of evil workers, beware of the concision. ³For we are the circumcision, which worship God in the Spirit, and rejoice in Christ Jesus, and have no confidence in the flesh. ⁴Though I might also have confidence in the flesh. If any other man thinketh that he hath whereof he might trust in the flesh, I more: ⁵circumcised the eighth day, of the stock of Israel, of the tribe of Benjamin, a Hebrew of the Hebrews; as touching the law, a Pharisee; ⁶concerning zeal, persecuting the church; touching the righteousness which is in the law, blameless. ⁷But what things were gain to me, those I counted loss for Christ. ⁸Yea doubtless, and I count all things but loss for the excellency of the knowledge of Christ Jesus my Lord: for whom I have suffered the loss of all things, and do count them as dung, that I may win*

Christ, ⁹and be found in Him, not having my own righteousness, which is from the law, but that which is through the faith of Christ, the righteousness which is of God by faith; ¹⁰that I may know Him, and the power of His resurrection, and the fellowship of His sufferings, being made conformable unto His death, ¹¹if, by any means, I might attain unto the resurrection of the dead. ¹²Not as though I had already attained, either were already perfect; but I follow after, if that I may apprehend that for which also I am apprehended of Christ Jesus. ¹³Brethren, I count not myself to have apprehended: but this one thing I do, forgetting those things which are behind, and reaching forth unto those things which are before, ¹⁴I press toward the mark for the prize of the high calling of God in Christ Jesus. (KJV)

As I began to study this chapter I paused for a moment, bowed my self-righteous head and asked God to confirm that this was the direction He wanted me to take for this meeting. After praying I looked up and there was our dog Rex standing in front of me.

At this point I reiterate that God has a sense of humor and, when you ask Him to, He knows how to get His point across. Remember that I prayed for an answer? Was Rex there to deliver it to me on God's behalf?

Well, Rex looked up at me, turned around and did the "doggy doo hunch." That's right. He dropped a DUNG PILE at my feet including all the aroma with it. Then he hit the bricks back down the stairs and left me with the mess!

Instantly, the verses Paul wrote **were emblazoned in my mind.** Here again are those verses:

> *Philippians 3:8-9 Yea doubtless, and I count all things but loss for the excellency of the knowledge of Jesus my Lord: <u>for whom I have suffered the loss of all things, and do count them but dung,</u> that I may win Christ, ⁹and be found in Him, <u>not having mine own righteousness</u>, which is of the law, but that*

which is through the faith of Christ, the righteousness which is of God by faith. (KJV) (emphasis mine)

Yes, God confirms His direction for you with His Holy Spirit's presence but He also confirms His word with *signs* as we see in:

Mark 16:20 And they went forth and preached everywhere, the Lord working with them, and confirming the word with signs following. Amen. (KJV)

Oh, by the way, my middle name is **REX**. Yep, Gregory **REX** Addie. I think the metaphor is self-explanatory here. Laughing out Loud.

When Physical Health is Not Desired

In the four New Testament Gospels and throughout the epistles of Paul in the Bible we see Jesus Christ and His ambassadors praying for health-challenged sick people. So, as modern day ambassadors, it is only natural that we step out in faith and pray for these burdened souls to have physical relief.

During my years in the water treatment business, I have had the opportunity to pray with many people inside their own homes. I try to be sensitive and available to anyone who has a sincere concern with which they need God's help. You would be surprised how people will open up to a perfect stranger rather than to their own spouse, friend or minister. I always try to keep in mind God's view about hurting or sick people:

1 Peter 5:6-7 6Therefore humble yourselves under the might hand of God, that He may exalt you in due time 7casting all your care upon Him, for He cares for you.

One day when I arrived at a home to do some repair work on their water treatment equipment I noticed that most of the family members were there and the mood was somewhat somber. I had known this family for quite some time. While working inside the mechanical room, the lady of the house (we will call her Penny) came into the room to see how I was doing. Casually I commented that it looked like they had a houseful for the weekend.

Penny's countenance immediately became downcast for a moment before she responded. She told me that her husband (whom we will call Orwell) had been diagnosed with cancer and had just been told by his doctor that he had only six months to live. With much empathy I told her that I was a Christian lay minister and that I would be more than happy to pray with Orwell and believe that God would heal him.

Penny went and got Orwell who told me they were Lutherans. First, I asked him if he was at peace with the Lord concerning his eternal salvation through Jesus Christ. He said he had been in touch with his pastor and he was mentally and scripturally at peace with his convictions.

Then I asked him if he would like me to pray for him. He said he would appreciate that. So, I began the prayer with Scripture that supported biblical healing to extend his time on this earth. As I prayed though, I did not sense the Holy Spirit's presence or the anointing to heal the sick that accompanies this line of prayer.

I stopped praying and asked Orwell what his desires were and for him to tell me what HE WOULD LIKE ME TO AGREE WITH HIM IN PRAYER. His answer was not the typical response. Orwell said that he really did not want to wait six months or longer to pass on. He said he did not want his wife, children and friends to watch him wither away with the cancer. He continued to say that he had had a good life and wanted to pass as soon as the Lord would take him. In my mind I thought how unselfish was this man to not want more time but rather less painful memories for his loved ones to bear after his eventual passing.

Taking Orwell's hand I prayed the promise prayer of agreement found in:

Matthew 18:19 *"Again I say to you that if two of you agree on earth concerning anything that they ask, it will be done for them by My Father in heaven."*

Together we prayed for him to pass on sooner rather than later for the benefit of his kin. That was on a Thursday. The following Tuesday I received a phone call from Penny to tell me Orwell had passed the day before, just four days after we had prayed together. She said they had gone to the doctor for a scheduled visit and were sitting in the waiting room. She had looked over at Orwell who appeared to be sleeping with his head slumped forward on his chest. Upon trying to wake him, she discovered that he had died and passed over into the Lord Jesus' hands.

Through this experience I learned a valuable lesson. Now I do not assume everyone wants to be **healed** before I pray for them. I have made it a point to ask people what their heart's desire is **BEFORE** I open my beak in prayer.

A Repeat Confirmation

It was not too long after the Orwell experience that something very similar occurred. This time it was with a Christian man who had asked me to come to his place of business to fix his water well's rotten egg smelling sulphur water.

When I walked into his business location two of the employees looked distressed. I heard one of the female employees ask the owner how they were going to pay some outstanding bills. Another employee commented on what they were planning to do if they lost their current job. As I listened to them, the owner approached me and asked how he could fix their water problem. He was concerned that the employees did not have decent water for consumption.

My vehicle was parked just outside his business window and he had noticed the business logo on my truck that read, "In**T**egrity Water Solutions." Many Christian businesses put a little fish symbol (<///><) after their business name to denote their Christian affiliation. In my business name, I made the first "t" in integrity triple the font size in a distinctive red color to denote the empty cross of Jesus Christ.

When he noticed this symbolism the owner asked if I was a Christian. I replied that I was and that I was more than happy to be of service to him in treating his water problem or I would answer any question concerning my vehicle's logo. He said that he was a believer in Jesus Christ as well. He quickly changed the subject from water treatment to personal hardships.

He went on a full-scale verbal "brain and battered soul heart dump." I remember him telling me of multiple surgeries he had undergone, financial woes, employee problems, pending bankruptcies and other hardships that seemed to have no end.

Instead of jumping in and offering a Godly rescue via prayer I asked him what I could do to help him. He then asked me to pray for him. I asked what he would like <u>specifically</u> for God to do. He said, "ALL I WANT IS PEACE." I could well understand that request as I could not even image how to pray for the many facets of his messed up world. So, like in the Orwell story, I prayed the ***Matthew 18:19*** prayer of agreement with him.

About a month later I stopped in to see how he was doing. When I asked an employee how the business owner was, she told me he had died two weeks earlier. I remembered that my prayer with him was for "peace" and that is exactly what God gave him.

Our Ultimate Healing

Psalm 116:15 Precious in the sight of the Lord is the death of His saints.

2 Corinthians 5:1-8 For we know that if our earthly house, this tent, is destroyed, we have a building from God, a house not made with hands, eternal in the heavens. ²For in this we groan, earnestly desiring to be clothed with our habitation which is from heaven, ³if indeed, having been clothed, we shall not be found naked. ⁴For we who are in this tent groan, being burdened, not because we want to be unclothed, but further clothed, that mortality may be swallowed up by life. ⁵Now He who has prepared us for this very thing is God, who also has given us the Spirit as a guarantee. ⁶So we are always confident, knowing that while we are at home in the body we are absent from the Lord. ⁷For we walk by faith, not by sight. ⁸We are confident, yes, well pleased rather to be absent from the body and to be present with the Lord.

Philippians 1: 21-23 ²¹For to me, to live is Christ, and to die is gain. ²²But if I live on in the flesh, this will mean fruit from my labor; yet what I shall choose I cannot tell. ²³For I am hard-pressed between the two, having a desire to depart and be with Christ, which is far better.

Wild Bull

It was late on a Thursday night and I was on my last residential water softener repair service call of the day. We will call this resident "Wild Bull." Upon entering his house, Wild Bull was sitting at his table sucking down a beer and it was apparent that he had noticed my truck logo that read, "In**T**egrity Water Solutions" with the "T" in the logo being triple sized font so that it looks like a biblical cross.

Before I could ask him where his water softener unit was, Wild Bull bellowed out, " I don't believe there is a God." I was taken aback as it was out of the norm to have someone just fire that out at you as soon as you walked through their door.

In response, I smiled and introduced myself. I asked him if he would like me to work on his water softener first or give him my thoughts as to why there is a God. He directed me to his basement and I repaired his water softener. By doing the water softener repair first, it gave me time to think through the response I wanted to give him in the defense that there truly is a God.

After finishing the repair I went back upstairs and asked if I could sit down with him. He agreed. I sat down and asked him why he did not think there is a God. His response was kind of different. His reasoning for not believing that there is a God was because he could not have dreams in his sleep. He said that because of this he was always in a state of unrest.

Instead of giving him the usual "Romans Road" biblical scriptures and starting a debate, I asked him if he truly wanted to know for a fact that there is a God. I continued by saying, "There is a God that truly cares about your state of unrest" and, "He loves you regardless of your past or present situations." I then said, "Wild Bull, there is a Biblical scripture that says:

Matthew 18:19 Again, truly I tell you that if two of you on earth agree about anything they ask for, it will be done for them by my Father in heaven."

I told him that if he would "agree with me," God would show him that there is a God, a God that loves him, and a God that would provide the answers that he sought according to the words Jesus had spoken and were recorded in Scripture. Then I extended my hand across the table and said, "Wild Bull, if you agree with this request, allow me to pray for you."

So, he stretched out his hand across the table and took my hand. I prayed that God would confirm this biblical Scripture by whatever means God thought best and that God would show him that He loves him and had sent Jesus to give him the kind of relief he was looking for.

After praying I got up from the table and thanked him for allowing me to service his water softener but also for giving me an opportunity to show him that there is a God. As I drove away from his house that night, I was very unsettled and had a big ole' gut check about what had just transpired. This "gut check" meant that the Holy Spirit was telling me there was something very critical about this situation that I was not seeing or understanding.

When this happens to me, I resort to prayer, not just a verbal prayer in English, but a prayer in the Spirit. Now for those of you who are not familiar with praying in the Spirit or praying in tongues, I will give you some biblical references for the power of doing this. The Bible says in:

> *1 Corinthians 14:2 For anyone who speaks in a tongue does not speak to people but to God. Indeed, no one understands them; they utter mysteries by the Spirit. (NIV)*

> *Ephesians 6:18 And pray in the Spirit on all occasions with all kinds of prayers and requests. With this in mind, be alert and always keep on praying for all the Lord's people. (NIV)*

> *Jude 1:20-21 [20]But you, dear friends, by building yourselves up in your most holy faith and praying in the Holy Spirit, [21]keep yourselves in God's love as you wait for the mercy of our Lord Jesus Christ to bring you to eternal life. (NIV)*

> *1 Corinthians 14:14 For if I pray in a tongue, my spirit prays, but my mind is unfruitful. (NIV)*

All the way home I prayed *in the Spirit* for Wild Bull because I knew there was something alarming about the reason for my being at his home that night.

Fast forward to a couple of months after this happened. I was driving down the road and received a phone call. Guess who? That's right! It was Wild Bull calling me. I answered the phone with ,

"InTegrity Water Solutions – this is Greg." The voice on the other end responded, "Hello, is this Greg Addie?" I replied, "Yes, how may I help you?" The airways went silent for a moment. Then the voice said, "Greg, this is Wild Bull." Another long pause of quiet air space followed. Then in an emotional cracked voice Wild Bull said, "God is my Co-Pilot."

I asked, "Hello, Bull. Why in the world would you say 'God is my Co-pilot?'" Wild Bull went on to tell me his harrowing story, a story that would answer my question about why I had had such a big time gut check in my spirit after I left his house that Thursday night.

A little side note here. For those of you who have been baptized in the Spirit, this should give you a reflective urgency as to why you need to immediately pray in the Spirit when God is trying to warn you about an event that will take place. These types of events may be about yourself, your family, your friends, a political situation or anything that God, the Holy Spirit, has chosen you to address, at that moment, in the unseen realm of the Spirit.

I can tell you from hundreds of my own experiences of praying in "the Spirit," that if you submit, and take the five to twenty minutes needed to address a situation, God will show you in the future what that was all about.

2 Chronicles 16:9 *9For the eyes of the Lord run to and fro throughout the whole earth, to show Himself strong on behalf of those whose heart is loyal to Him. (KJV)*

Wild Bull went on to tell me that the day following my Thursday night prayer, he and his boys went up to the northern Wisconsin ATV (All-Terrain Vehicle) trails to have some fun. He said that while riding his ATV he lost control and went over a cliff.

He and the ATV rolled together all the way to the bottom where he lost consciousness. He told me that when they found him, his face was a deathly grayish purple. By the time the ambulance arrived, a good half hour had passed with no resuscitation. Many of you reading this know that our brain will begin to die after six minutes of oxygen deprivation.

Somehow the paramedics were able to resuscitate him on the way to the hospital. When Wild Bull regained consciousness one of the first things he remembered was the prayer we had prayed just the night before. He said it occurred to him that God had just answered that prayer by saving his life and giving him more time to live.

I replied, "Wild Bull, you have just been given a great gift. Most people do not get a second chance and end up in eternal Hell because they did not accept God's gift of eternal life through Jesus Christ." Wild Bull asked, "Greg, would you go to church with me?" I said, "Of course I will, Bull." Little did I know that he had already picked out and had been to a church near his home.

When I met him at the church the next Sunday, I was surprised to find that God had set him up in the most **NON-Religious** atmosphere that one could find. This church was an old movie theater. They still used the old seats that have the cup holders and still served popcorn and drinks before the service. PERFECT!!!

The church was non-denominational with a relaxed come-as-you-are acceptance. Their order of service was basic evangelical with praise and worship preceding a biblical message. I knew this would be a good place for Wild Bull to get a good rudimentary foundation. I at one more time with him and then let the Holy Spirit take it from there. Laughing out loud, like the Holy Spirit needed MY help at this point.

A Facebook Challenge

During the writing of this book I took a break and went "Facebooking." I posted a quick comment on my wall that read, "I am convinced that God is good ALL OF THE TIME." One of the comments I received was this. "OK, I have a question or two. If God is always good, then sometimes we His children must have misunderstood some of His teachings. For example, when He kicked

Adam and Eve out of the Garden, was that good? Maybe sometimes a bad thing is required so the right thing can be accomplished. There are numerous examples of being commanded to do something we His children believe is bad. Sacrifice a son. Bad. Needed in order to save all the rest of His children. Good. I suggest that if God has been good to you and you say 'God has been good to me,' then that is probably a truthful statement. But to say 'God is always good' would be a false statement. God will never sin or He would cease to be God but He isn't always good."

I replied, "If you try to understand God on a horizontal level and not on a vertical plane, you will think God is unjust. A horizontal view of God is that which is seen within the sphere and reality of the earth we live in day to day. This reality was not derived from God but by man's own free will choices.

"The Bible says that by one original sin of one man, Adam, that ALL men were made sinful and unholy and will die. However, the Bible also says by the righteousness of One Man namely, Jesus Christ, ALL men can be made holy and without sin apart from their own works. And, if they see God on a vertical plane, that is - an upward eternal level, they can receive the eternal provisions He has made for free-willed man.

"You will see that through the sacrifice of this God-Man, Jesus, God offers eternal life for all who will simply ask for it. Jesus Himself stated, 'IN THIS LIFE YOU WILL HAVE TROUBLE' - (horizontal realm) but then Jesus immediately went on to say, 'BUT TAKE HEART, FOR I HAVE OVERCOME THE WORLD' (eternal vertical upward level). Therefore, God is good ALL THE TIME. For it is man's actions that caused all these bad things to occur in this life. MAN CURSED HIMSELF AT THE GARDEN OF EDEN BY BREAKING ONE SIMPLE GODLY COMMAND - do not eat the fruit of the tree of the knowledge of good and evil.

"If God had not removed Adam and Eve from the Garden of Eden, they would have died instantly the next time He came to the Garden to walk with them. WHY? Because the Bible says in:

Romans 6:23 *For the wages of sin is DEATH but the gift of God is eternal life in Christ Jesus our Lord.*

"In other words, HE SAVED THEIR LIVES BY REMOVING THEM FROM HIS HOLY PRESENCE.

"It is kind of like keeping Kryptonite away from Superman in order to save him. Even though Superman came from Krypton, he would die if he came in contact with his place of birth and origin, JUST LIKE ANY MAN WILL DO WHO TRIES TO COME TO GOD 'THE ORIGINAL CREATOR' APART FROM JESUS. You see, Jesus, because He is God *and* Man, could take the sinful part of man upon the God part of Himself and cleanse it to save us from our Kryptonite called Sin.

"I asked Jesus into my life thirty-five years ago and I am writing a book about the multiple miracles I have seen God work in His kindness towards mankind."

FILL 'R UP

One day late in 2009 I was driving my work van toward Delavan, Wisconsin. Down the road I could see on my right hand side a Shell gas station with a convenience store attached to it. **As I approached it, I could tangibly sense and feel the Holy Spirit's presence around me**. Sensing the presence of God's Holy Spirit has always been a sign for me to pay attention to what is going on around me because He has something He would like to accomplish at the moment.

I pulled into the gas station and decided to top off my gas tank. As I was standing by my vehicle a small car pulled up a few pumps away. A young blond gal in a nurse's uniform got out and I could see she was wiping tears out of her eyes.

After I finished filling up my vehicle I went inside the convenience store to pay for my fuel. As I approached the cashier I noticed that he was of Middle Eastern descent. On the counter there was a small TV and on it I could see a prayer tower and could hear someone chanting prayers from its steeple to the people below who were bowing over their prayer rugs in the traditional Islamic prayer position. So, I assumed this cashier was Muslim as well. I handed him my credit card and he rang up the sale.

As he was processing my card, I noticed the young blonde gal outside was crying again but trying to regain her composure before she came inside. I signed my fuel receipt and asked the cashier the cost of the gasoline for the little car out front. He looked and said, "Three dollars." Three bucks at that time bought less than one gallon of gas.

Just about then it occurred to me what my mission was in stopping at this gas station. The young blonde gal walked in. I stopped her before she got to the cashier and said, "Hello, my name is Greg and I noticed you were a little distraught while getting your gasoline. Would you do me a favor? Go back to your vehicle and FILL'R up with gas and I will pay for it."

In a voice loud enough for the Muslim man to hear, I continued by saying that God had asked me to stop at this gas station because HE had someone that HE wanted to help. Then I said, "You will do me a great honor by letting me be obedient to God by paying for your full tank of fuel."

No more had the words left my mouth than she burst into tears and held her face in her hands. She said, "I just lost my job and I do not have enough gas or money to make it back home." She continued, "I prayed to God before I pulled in here for Him to help me." I told her that I was there to answer her prayer and help her get home safely. So, she went back outside to continue filling up her car.

Then I turned and faced the now very wide-eyed cashier. Again I handed him my credit card and asked him to put her gasoline purchase on it. When the young blonde was finished filling her vehicle, he did just as I requested. As the young lady was making her way back into the store I felt that the Holy Spirit wanted me to pass on one more piece of information to her.

When she returned to the store I looked her straight in the eyes and said, "God wants me to tell you something." With a smile, she listened intently as I said, "God wants you to know that He is a **PRO**moter and not a **DE**moter. If you lost this job, it is because God has something much bigger and much better waiting for you in the very near future." I continued, "He wants you to know that He loves you very, very much and is well pleased with you."

With that said she gave me a big ole hug. The cashier reached out his hand and gave me a handshake. I said to him, "Remember, Jesus Christ loves YOU as well." Then I walked out the door, got into my van and left.

Sometimes I wish I could see into the future about that encounter. It would be nice to know what the young nurse finally did with her life and what impact was made on the Muslim man that day. I guess, like many other things in life, I will just have to wait to find out until I stand before the Judgment Seat of Christ.

Oh, yes. I do not want to be remiss in letting you know what the Judgment Seat of Christ is all about. There are two judgments for mankind. One is for those who **accept** Jesus Christ as their Lord and Savior and the other is for those who **reject** Jesus Christ and His Gospel.

The first one for believers is conducted after the Second Coming of Jesus Christ which will be after the seven-year period of the Great Tribulation. The second one is called the Great White Throne

Judgment for those who never accepted Jesus Christ for their salvation. I will give you Bible references for both.

First, as to the Judgment Seat of Christ, I have always considered this judgement to be like a sports banquet for those who have run the race of life for Jesus Christ and have received salvation through Him. Paul makes mention of this as follows:

> ***1 Corinthians 9:24** Do you not know that those who run in a race all run, but one receives the prize? Run in such a way that you may obtain it.*

The Judgment Seat of Christ

Paul writes of the Judgment Seat of Christ in his letter to the Romans:

> ***Romans 14:10-12** **10** But why do you judge your brother? Or why do you show contempt for your brother? For we shall all stand before the judgment seat of Christ. **11** For it is written: "As I live, says the Lord, every knee shall bow to Me, and every tongue shall confess to God." **12** So then each of us shall give account of himself to God.*

> ***2 Corinthians 5:1-21** For we know that if our earthly house, this tent, is destroyed, we have a building from God, a house not made with hands, eternal in the heavens. **2** For in this we groan, earnestly desiring to be clothed with our habitation which is from heaven, **3** if indeed, having been clothed, we shall not be found naked. **4** For we who are in this tent groan, being burdened, not because we want to be unclothed, but further clothed, that mortality may be swallowed up by life. **5** Now He who has prepared us for this very thing is God, who also has given us the Spirit as a guarantee. **6** So we are always confident, knowing that while we are at home in the body, we are absent from the Lord. **7** For we walk by faith, not by sight. **8** We are*

confident, yes, well pleased rather to be absent from the body and to be present with the Lord.

The Judgment Seat of Christ

[9] Therefore we make it our aim, whether present or absent, to be well pleasing to Him. [10] For we must all appear before the judgment seat of Christ, that each one may receive the things done in the body, according to what he has done, whether good or bad. [11] Knowing, therefore, the terror of the Lord, we persuade men; but we are well known to God, and I also trust are well known in your consciences.

Be Reconciled to God

[12] For we do not commend ourselves again to you, but give you opportunity to boast on our behalf, that you may have an answer for those who boast in appearance and not in heart. [13] For if we are beside ourselves, it is for God; or if we are of sound mind, it is for you. [14] For the love of Christ compels us, because we judge thus: that if One died for all, then all died; [15] and He died for all, that those who live should live no longer for themselves, but for Him who died for them and rose again. [16] Therefore, from now on, we regard no one according to the flesh. Even though we have known Christ according to the flesh, yet now we know Him thus no longer. [17] Therefore, if anyone is in Christ, he is a new creation; old things have passed away; behold, all things have become new. [18] Now all things are of God, who has reconciled us to Himself through Jesus Christ, and has given us the ministry of reconciliation, [19] that is, that God was in Christ reconciling the world to Himself, not imputing their trespasses to them, and has committed to us the word of reconciliation. [20] Now then, we are ambassadors for Christ, as though God were pleading through us: we implore

you on Christ's behalf, be reconciled to God. [21]For He made Him who knew no sin to be sin for us, that we might become the righteousness of God in Him.

Revelation 20:4-6 [4]And I saw thrones, and they sat on them, and judgment was committed to them. Then I saw the souls of those who had been beheaded for their witness to Jesus and for the word of God, who had not worshiped the beast or his image, and had not received his mark on their foreheads or on their hands. And they lived and reigned with Christ for a thousand years. [5]But the rest of the dead did not live again until the thousand years were finished. This is the first resurrection. [6]Blessed and holy is he who has part in the first resurrection. Over such the second death has no power, but they shall be priests of God and of Christ and shall reign with Him a thousand years.

The GREAT WHITE THRONE JUDGEMENT

Now, *this* is one place that YOU DO NOT WANT TO BE JUDGED!! Here is why:

Revelation 20:11-15 [11]Then I saw a great white throne and Him who sat on it, from whose face the earth and the heaven fled away. And there was found no place for them. [12]And I saw the dead, small and great, standing before God, and books were opened. And another book was opened, which is the Book of Life. And the dead were judged according to their works, by the things that were written in the books. [13]The sea gave up the dead who were in it, and Death and Hades delivered up the dead who were in them. And they were judged, each one according to his works. [14]Then Death and Hades were cast into the lake of fire. This is the second death. [15]And anyone not found written in the Book of Life was cast into the lake of fire.

The Burning House

During my time in the water treatment business, I have met many interesting people. Some of these people are non-Christians, some are BNO (By Name Only) Christians, and others are true believers in the Gospel of Jesus Christ.

I have found that most true believing Christians fall into several categories within their walk of faith. Some are introverted private believers who have a love for God through Jesus but are content with their work life and going to church just on Sundays and/or holidays.

Others are active within their church body but shy away from propagating the Gospel outside their church environment. Still others feel called by God to reach out to those who have yet to believe in Jesus Christ and His eternal message of peace.

It is not my intent to categorize these folks in order to judge their works for God. What every believer does is between them and the Holy Spirit. I always try to keep in mind my United States Marine Corps (USMC) service days. Statistically, when one is in a war, only about 25% actually do the fighting. The rest are in support of the front line warriors. During a war, you need people to strategize, people to administrate, people to keep communications flowing, people to train troops, people to fight, people to supply, people to cook and ALL ARE NECCESARY TO WIN.

In the Christian realm, we see the apostle Paul categorize the five main jobs of people who feel they are called to "down-to-earth where the rubber meets the road" kinds of service for God. We see this in:

> ***Ephesians 4:1-16** I, therefore, the prisoner of the Lord, beseech you to walk worthy of the calling with which you were called, **2**with all lowliness and gentleness, with longsuffering, bearing with one another in love, **3**endeavoring to keep the unity of the Spirit in the bond of peace. **4**There is one body and one Spirit, just as you were called in one hope of your calling; **5**one Lord,*

one faith, one baptism; ⁶one God and Father of all, who is above all, and through all, and in you all.

Spiritual Gifts

⁷But to each one of us grace was given according to the measure of Christ's gift. ⁸Therefore He says: "When He ascended on high, He led captivity captive, And gave gifts to men." ⁹(Now this, "He ascended"— what does it mean but that He also first descended into the lower parts of the earth? ¹⁰He who descended is also the One who ascended far above all the heavens, that He might fill all things.) ¹¹And He himself gave some to be apostles, some prophets, some evangelists, and some pastors and teachers, ¹²for the equipping of the saints for the work of ministry, for the edifying of the body of Christ, ¹³ till we all come to the unity of the faith and of the knowledge of the Son of God, to a perfect man, to the measure of the stature of the fullness of Christ; ¹⁴ that we should no longer be children, tossed to and fro and carried about with every wind of doctrine, by the trickery of men, in the cunning craftiness of deceitful plotting, ¹⁵ but, speaking the truth in love, may grow up in all things into Him who is the head - Christ - ¹⁶from whom the whole body, joined and knit together by what every joint supplies, according to the effective working by which every part does its share, causes growth of the body for the edifying of itself in love.

Now, within these five callings, and for the purpose of this story, I would like to focus on the "evangelist." I have found there are two types of evangelists out there spreading and attempting to propagate the Gospel.

The first type I will call 'seasoned and matured.' This group of people is normally made up of seasoned believers who have experienced the grace of God, who have tasted and seen that the Lord is good, who have understood the Grace of God taught within Paul's Gospel letters and who have learned only to open their mouths as directed by the Holy Spirit and not out of fleshly self-fulfilling obligation. Their messages to the unbeliever are messages of hope; that by believing in the Gospel of Jesus Christ one day they too will hear Jesus say to them these words:

> *Matthew 25:21 "His master replied, 'Well done, good and faithful servant! You have been faithful with a few things; I will put you in charge of many things. Come and share your master's happiness!' (NIV)*

The second type I will call 'those who lack or just plain ignore' the above criteria and normally follow zealously Judao Old Testament teaching and who mix in New Testament writings from Peter and Jude. Below are some confirming passages that Paul the apostle wrote concerning mixing of old Covenant (Old Testament) and new Covenant (New Testament) tenets of faith together:

> *2 Corinthians 3:13 We are not like Moses, who would put a veil over his face to prevent the Israelites from seeing the end of what was passing away. (NIV)*

> *2 Corinthians 3:14 But their minds were made dull, for to this day the same veil remains when the old covenant is read. It has not been removed, because only in Christ is it taken away. (NIV)*

> *2 Corinthians 3:15 Even to this day when Moses is read, a veil covers their hearts. (NIV)*

> *2 Corinthians 3:16 But whenever anyone turns to the Lord, the veil is taken away.(NIV)*

By doing so, this type of evangelist will attempt to convert the lost by fear, manipulation, and hell fire and brimstone teaching. Their message to the unbeliever is an ultimatum that by not accepting the Gospel of Jesus Christ they will hear Jesus say to them:

Matthew 25:41 "Then He will say to those on His left, 'Depart from Me, you who are cursed, into the eternal fire prepared for the devil and his angels. (NIV)

Though their message IS NOT FALSE, it tends to NOT convince people to convert to faith in Jesus Christ.

This segment is focused on an individual believer I met in my journey who normally followed the second type of evangelism. We will call him "Pal."

Pal and I met when I was supplying water treatment equipment for a 200+ condominium project. It was a good-sized project and I had the God-given opportunity to talk with each new condominium owner about their water quality and sometimes a little bit about Jesus Christ. Pal was one of those new condominium owners who immediately noticed the Christian fish logo on my work van. It did not take long for Pal to give me his version of the Gospel which conformed to my second type of evangelist description. So, I knew God had sent me to Pal to possibly provide some friendship and Bible teaching that would dull his aggressive hell fire and brimstone message a tad. Perhaps I could also help sharpen his biblical grace knowledge so he could become a winner of souls by love and not by baseball bat.

Many hours were spent stopping by his condominium as I was meeting with the other new owners on the project. It must have worked because he started telling people on the project that I was his new pastor and that they should listen to what I had to say about Jesus. For this I can thank him.

Pal was an older gentleman and began to have heart issues. Eventually, he was in the hospital with heart failure and was given just days to live. It was during that time that I got to say goodbye to Pal and, with the Holy Spirit's help, assured him of his eternal salvation based on the grace of God and his core belief in the Gospel of Jesus Christ.

Pal asked me to officiate at his funeral and to give a Gospel message that reminded people that there was a HELL after death for those who did not believe in Jesus Christ. I told him I would do this for him. The last Scripture I read to him was from **Revelation 21**. I encourage you to read this chapter yourself but the main passage I read to console him was where the apostle John writes:

> ***Revelation 21:4-5*** *⁴And God will wipe away every tear from their eyes; there shall be no more death, nor sorrow, nor crying. There shall be no more pain, for the former things have passed away." ⁵Then He who sat on the throne said, "Behold, I make all things new." And He said to me, "Write, for these words are true and faithful."*

Shortly after I spent this evening with Pal, I received word from his family that he had passed. The date for the wake and funeral service was set. I began to search my soul for the proper eulogy that would include Pal's request for a hell fire and brimstone salvation message.

The day of the funeral came very quickly. These types of presentations always seem to come too quickly because it is not always easy to prepare a speech or message on a subject that goes against your normal low-key mode of reaching out to people.

The funeral location was about an hour's drive from my house. While I traveled I began to pray and I asked God for the wisdom and the words to convey to the people there that, without Jesus Christ in one's life, the reality of an eternal hell is inevitable.

As I drove down Interstate 43, I noticed a thick column of black smoke ahead of me. As I got closer, I could see a house on fire that was off on a small side road close to the interstate. An old two-story farmhouse was totally engulfed in flames. I saw fire trucks, EMT vehicles and police cars. Most of the vehicles must have just arrived as their red, blue and yellow lights were still flashing. From the elevated height of the interstate I could see the firemen trying to douse the flames with water. Other firemen had surrounded the house looking for anyone that needed to be rescued from the flames blasting through the windows. It was obvious that, if there was anyone in that house, they had surely met an unexpected fiery fate.

There it was!! In that fiery scene was my message for the masses. As I continued down the road the Holy Spirit began to piece together that burning house with Scripture verses to turn it into a meaningful grace-filled salvation message.

The Message

As I began the eulogy, I told those gathered there that I had just experienced a scene that would have made Pal's normal Gospel message to them a reality while on this earth - a fire and brimstone house fire!! Many laughed or snickered when I said that, as they had been the recipients of Pal's historically aggressive message of hell fire. So, I told them the story of the fire that I just described and tempered into the story some allegorical meanings.

I told the crowd that what Pal had been preaching was true according to Biblical writings by Jesus' apostles. However, I wanted them to see *who* was there at the fire as well.

There were *firemen* looking inside the burning house trying to find any signs of life before the fire reached them. I told them that God will send people and His Holy Spirit to every one of us to convince our hearts to believe in the death, burial and resurrection of Jesus Christ before hell's fire can touch us individually.

Then I told them that He has an *ambulance* waiting right outside our scorched heart's door to give us a message of His great love and grace. The ambulance is called the *Bible* and it is packed with the healing salve of God's written word to each one of us.

Around your house or heart, I continued, God has also placed His *policemen*. These are unseen angels He sends to keep premature harm from coming to you until you have had a chance to make a CHOICE of where you will spend eternity.

To conclude my message, I shared some details of Pal's military service history, the fatherly responsibilities at which he had excelled and then I thanked his wife Mary for all the years of love, service and care she had given him. I finished with a prayer and a personal invitation for anyone there to accept Jesus right where they sat. After the service the family came up to me and said that I (actually, the Holy Spirit) had hit the nail on the head about their dad and that was exactly the kind of message he would have wanted.

The Holy Spirit's Inexhaustible Works

John 21: 24-25 *²⁴This is the disciple who testifies to these things and who wrote them down. We know that his testimony is true. (NIV)*

²⁵ Jesus did many other things as well. If every one of them were written down, I suppose that even the whole world would not have room for the books that would be written.

I wanted to share this verse at the end of this chapter as I could add endless more pages to this book telling all the different things Jesus has done in my life through the Holy Spirit. Examples I could add are:

- The hundreds of times I have felt His presence in music that sent cleansing healing tears down my face.
- The times He gave me what to say when confronted by "know it all, arrogant religious" people and cults.
- The times He gut-checked me to stay out of certain areas of thought that were enticing my flesh toward unclean, angry or unproductive works.

- The times He has sent "word pictures" to me that there was an LEO (Law Enforcement Officer) just over the next hill to save me a ticket and insurance increase. Just to be clear, if He continually must warn you like this, He will allow you to get a citation for not listening to Him! Yes, discipline is on its way when you continually buck the Holy Spirit and grieve Him.

- The times that He has brought a national situation to my mind or a political figure for whom He wants me to pray.

- The numerous times He would give me countless ways and places to leave Gospel tracts. My favorite tracts are found at https://www.chick.com/ "Back From The Dead?" or "This Was Your Life."

- The times that He has shown me a person who was sitting alone in a car, in a restaurant or next to me on an airplane who needed wisdom, encouragement or salvation (like in the "Fill 'R Up" story).

- The several times that He has warned me of potential personal harm from demonically influenced people and would have me carry CCW (Concealed Carry Weapon) that day only to have a situation manifest that could have been harmful or deadly to myself or others.

- The literally hundreds of times He has opened up a door of discussion about the Gospel of Jesus Christ when I went on a service call or product delivery.

- The list is endless when I keep recalling my past in my mind.

Finally, as a conclusion to this chapter, I want to mention this verse:

John 14:12. *"Most assuredly, I say to you, <u>he who believes in Me</u>, the works that I do he will do also; and greater works than these <u>he will do</u>, because I go to My Father. (emphasis mine)*

Gregory Addie

Chapter 6

Going for the Gold

Hurriedly, each man ran for his tools. Like bucks during rut, everyone ran for a plot of ground that he could claim as his own for a call had been sounded that precious gold had been found and each man wanted his just due.

Among these treasure seekers there was a man who had great expectations for his claim. He sold all that he had in order to buy the land and tools needed to pursue the dreams which can make men earthly rich, worthwhile, valuable, and prestigious.

As he began to dig, he thought of all the things he would be able to buy with his gold. "Sky's the limit," he thought, as visions of beautiful Caribbean shores swam through his mind.

The man began to encounter many large stones as he dug, as each stone clanged against his shovel, he would reach down, examine it for worth, and throw it onto a pile in the middle of the hole. He thought to himself, "What a bunch of worthless rocks in here. How will I ever be able to reach the height of my dreams with so many of them in my way?"

And so, the man dug and dug, harder and harder, deeper and deeper until he was utterly exhausted from hours of strenuous work. He sat down for a rest on the pile of worthless rocks in the middle of the now deep pit. With sweat pouring down his face, he thought, "Surely I had better climb out of this hole and get a drink of water or I will perish of thirst." The man got off the rock pile only to find that he had dug a hole so deep that he wondered if it was even possible to get out of it.

With walls of sand around him and a rock pile behind him, this thirsty and parched man began to attempt to climb out of his self-dug hole. However, due to the sandy walls he found that the more he tried to climb up the wall, the more the sand would cave in around his feet. After many hours of frustrating attempts to escape the pit, the man sat down and thought, "It is too hard to escape from this hole. How stupid of me <u>not to think this through before I began to dig</u>."

So, the man began to yell for help thinking that other treasure hunters were close by and could assist him in an escape. The man yelled and screamed with everything that was in him only to have his cries fall on deaf ears for all the other treasure hunters were so busy digging their own holes that they could not hear him.

Finally, with desperation filling his heart and a great thirst in his throat, he made a final call for help. "If there is a God in heaven, please show me the way out of this pit." With his strength exhausted, the man humbly sat back down on his rock pile in the middle of his hole.

Hopelessly, the man sat in silence and looked at the deep inescapable hole that he had dug for himself. As he sat there he noticed one of those worthless stones release itself from high up on the side of one of the sandy walls and it rolled to the bottom of the pit to his feet. He put his foot on the rock as if to smoosh it into the sand. However, the rock did not sink into the sand like his feet did earlier when he was attempting to climb out of the pit.

Suddenly, it dawned on him that the stone was like a foundation he could build upon. He reasoned that if he put the stones in front of him and up the sides of the wall, he may have a solid footing on which to climb to safety. The stones that he once deemed worthless had now become as precious as the gold he had sought in the first place and they could now become his salvation.

The man placed stone upon stone and escaped up this foundation of solid rock to the top of his pit. Once he reached the top he looked out across the gold field and saw that all the other treasure hunters had also dug great pits for themselves.

Going to each pit he saw that those other men had perished there. The man then remembered his final cry to God and realized that it was only because God had **allowed** him to see the rock roll down from above that he lived. It was because they had not seen the value of the rocks that all the others had perished.

Then in deep thought, the man recalled his experience and marked his pit with a memorial marker and this poem engraved upon it:

Rock Dream

*This pit was dug on a promise of gold
but all I found was a lie within my soul.*

*While in its depths my voice did scream
to God who saw me in this horrible dream.*

*His eyes did see my pitiful plight and
His merciful wings did go to flight.*

*For the pit was all around and
damnation by stagnation
in my soul did abound.*

*In His hands I was lifted up
and was not made to drink this bitter cup.*

*For in God's plan I now can see
That His timing was always perfect for me.*

*Gregory R. Addie
June 10, 2017*

Insights into GOING FOR THE GOLD Allegory

Years ago when I first wrote this story, I was going through a period in my life when gaining wealth was paramount above all things. It is easier now, decades later, for me to talk about it, after I have established a measure of wealth and can reflect on both sides of the wealth and little wealth coin.

Apostle Paul said on a similar note:

> ***Philippians 4:12-13*** *[12] I know how to be abased, and I know how to abound. Everywhere and in all things I have learned both to be full and to be hungry, both to abound and to suffer need. [13] I can do all things through Christ who strengthens me.*

I felt it was important to share the above allegory since the subject of gaining and possessing wealth can play a role in choosing to live under its *controlling* influence or obtaining eternal salvation.

Paul the apostle thought it was such an important topic that he wrote this:

> ***1 Timothy 6:10*** *For the <u>love of money</u> is a root of all kinds of evil, for which some have strayed from the faith in their greediness, and pierced themselves through with many sorrows. (emphasis mine)*

It is proper that we underscore the "LOVE OF MONEY" in that verse for many or all of us have some measure of wealth but it becomes problematic when we begin to love, covet and obsess over what money can do for us.

Jesus gives us an example of how being a rich influential person with the love of money can cost us our eternal life. Luke's account reads:

> ***Luke 18:18-25*** *[18] Now a certain ruler asked Him, "Good Teacher, what shall I do to inherit eternal life?" [19] So Jesus said*

to him, "Why do you call Me good? No one is good but One, that is, God. ²⁰You know the commandments: 'Do not commit adultery,' 'Do not murder,' 'Do not steal,' 'Do not bear false witness,' 'Honor your father and your mother.'" ²¹And he said (the rich young man), "All these things I have kept from my youth." ²²So when Jesus heard these things, He said to him, "You still lack one thing. Sell all that you have and distribute to the poor, and you will have treasure in heaven; and come, follow Me." ²³But when he heard this, he became very sorrowful, for he was very rich. ²⁴And when Jesus saw that he became very sorrowful, He said, "How hard it is for those who have riches to enter the kingdom of God! ²⁵For it is easier for a camel to go through the eye of a needle than for a rich man to enter the kingdom of God."*

Luke gives us another account of how money can be a religious trap and a salvation killer for power-hungry church leaders like our modern day "Name it and claim it" televangelists:

Luke 16: 14–15 ¹⁴Now the Pharisees, <u>who were lovers of money</u>, also heard all these things, and they derided Him. ¹⁵And He said to them, "You are those who justify yourselves before men, but God knows your hearts. <u>For what is highly esteemed among men is an abomination in the sight of God</u>." (emphasis mine)

Paul the apostle concludes this thought when he talks about <u>the "Last Days," yes, in which we live RIGHT NOW</u>:

2 Timothy 3: 1-5 But know this, that in the last days perilous times will come:²For men will be lovers of themselves, <u>lovers of money</u>, boasters, proud, blasphemers, disobedient to parents, unthankful, unholy, ³unloving, unforgiving, slanderers, without self-control, brutal, despisers of good, ⁴traitors, *headstrong, haughty, lovers of pleasure rather than lovers of God, ⁵having a form of godliness but denying its power. And from such people turn away! (emphasis mine)*

THE ALLEGORY EXPLAINED

Moving on now to our allegory - in this allegory we see a call go out to many men about the riches they may find on the earth. In the same way this world points to success with wealth being within this world, especially in AMERICA.

Many seek this kind of fulfillment by acquiring expensive degrees thinking that high paying jobs are an automatic result; new cars they cannot afford; and big homes with hefty mortgages. Before long they find they have dug themselves into a giant debt hole to which many become enslaved for the remainder of their lives.

While we are living this kind of lifestyle and are in a downward progression, God tends to put big rocks in our part of the earth we are working. These rocks are the good news of the Gospel of Jesus Christ, who is the eternal Rock of Salvation.

Most, like our allegorical man, will cast off the things of God like a worthless rock, not understanding that it is the very gold which their soul seeks and needs. Eternally speaking, it is actually fortunate when a man comes to the end of himself and cries out to God like this treasurer seeker did.

During my days on this earth, I have found that once a man does this, God is quick to bring His saving grace to bear. I can attest to this as I wrote earlier of my "Rock Dream." Remember:

Romans 10:13 "For whosoever calls upon the name of the Lord shall be saved."

As we saw in the allegory, the moment the man cried out to Him, God gave him the wisdom of accepting the pile of rocks, namely Jesus Christ, as his foundational pathway out of death's hole.

We see this in Scripture:

Psalm 50:15 Call upon Me in the day of trouble; <u>I will deliver you</u>, and you shall glorify Me."

Also in:

1 Corinthians 3:10 - 11 ***¹⁰ According to the grace of God, which was given to me, as a wise master builder I have laid the foundation, and another builds on it. But let each one take heed how he builds on it. ¹¹ For no other foundation can anyone lay than that which is laid, which is Jesus Christ.***

The man in the allegory got out of his earthly pit and was on his way to more eternal things as we note in his poem. Remember:

> *This pit was dug on a promise of gold*
> *but all I found was a lie within my soul.*
> *While in its depths my voice did scream*
> *to God who saw me in this horrible dream.*
> *His eyes did see my pitiful plight and*
> *His merciful wings did go to flight.*
> *For the pit was all around and*
> *damnation by stagnation*
> *in my soul did abound.*
> *In His hands, I was lifted up*
> *and was not made to drink this bitter cup.*
> *For in God's plan I now can see*
> *That His timing was always perfect for me.*
> *~ Gregory R. Addie ~*
> *June 10, 2017*

Also, please remember that after his escape the man went to all the holes dug by the other treasure seekers only to find death there. Two fitting Scriptures to end this allegory are found in:

Matthew 7:13-14 ¹³*"Enter by the narrow gate; for wide is the gate and broad is the way that leads to destruction, and there are many who go in by it.* ¹⁴*Because narrow is the gate and difficult is the way which leads to life, and there are few who find it.*

And in:

John 14:6 Jesus said to him, "I am the way, the truth, and the life. No one comes to the Father except through Me."

THE LOTTERY TICKET

In the late 1990s, I did an unthinkable act for a Christian. I bought a lottery ticket. To win the jackpot, this Wisconsin lottery ticket needed to have six matching numbers. Having less than six matching numbers reduced the prize value and the reward would be chump change.

So, the day after I bought this ticket, I was cruising down the road alternately looking up to drive and occasionally looking down at the ticket numbers to see if I had any matches. I quickly pulled over to the side of the road when I realized the first five numbers matched. I put my thumb over the last ticket number in a moment of surprised anticipation.

I thought, "If this last number matches, I will win the jackpot of THIRTEEN MILLION DOLLARS!" Yes, true story. Even after taxes I thought that I would still have about seven million dollars.

My mathematician brain kicked into high gear and I started calculating that each million at a 5% interest rate would yield an extra $50,000 annually for approximately $350,000 a year in interest as well. Then my heart started racing as I began to think of all the philanthropy I could do, let alone acquire a few new toys. Yes, I might even find freedom from my current employer as my ungrateful heart told him where he could stick his thirty pieces of silver.

The moment of truth was sitting under my thumb and I just HAD to know. I lifted my thumb off the sixth and final number. The winning number was 36. My sixth final number was………. 35!

AAAAAAARRRRRRGGGGGGGGG!! My mind screamed a loud "WHY, LORD?" You who used a 'lot' when it was cast in the Old Testament to decide issues had left me in a state of wanting answers.

Finally my mind settled down and I began to think about the disappointing financial loss. The first thought that came to mind was posed as a question to me. I thought, "If I had won all that loot, would I still be willing to take the time to personally sit in people's homes and share Jesus Christ's good Gospel of eternal life with them?" I honestly had to answer this still small voice with a "probably not like I am now."

The job I currently had was as an in-house residential sales representative. I shared the Gospel of Jesus Christ, prayed with sick people, schooled the unchurched or former churchgoers about the Gospel and grace truth versus dogmatic parasitical religion, and I saw many accept Jesus Christ as their sole answer to the eternal question of salvation that all of us must answer for ourselves.

The second question posed to me by this still small voice was "Is one person's eternal security worth thirteen million dollars?" I immediately answered with a resounding "NO!!" God really has a sense of humor, folks, for right after I answered the last mental question a song began going through my mind. It was a familiar one to me. It was sung by a group called KANSAS and was called "Carry On, Wayward Son." The lyrics went like this:

Carry On Wayward Son
recorded by Kansas

Carry on, my wayward son.
There'll be peace when you are done.

Gregory Addie

*Lay your weary head to rest.
Don't you cry no more.*

*Once I rose above the noise and confusion
Just to get a glimpse beyond the illusion.
I was soaring ever higher, but I flew too high.
Though my eyes could see I still was a blind man.
Though my mind could think I still was a mad man.
I hear the voices when I'm dreamin'.*

*I can hear them say, "Carry on, my wayward son.
There'll be peace when you are done.
Lay your weary head to rest.
Don't you cry no more."*

*Masquerading as a man with a reason,
My charade is the event of the season.
And if I claim to be a wise man, it surely means that I don't know.
On a stormy sea of moving emotion
Tossed about I'm like a ship on the ocean.
I set a course for winds of fortune, but I hear the voices say,*

*"Carry on, my wayward son.
There'll be peace when you are done.
Lay your weary head to rest.
Don't you cry no more.*

*Carry on, you will always remember.
Carry on, nothing equals the splendor.
Now your life's no longer empty.
Surely heaven waits for you.
Carry on, my wayward son.
There'll be peace when you are done.*

The Ambassador's Call
Lay your weary head to rest.
Don't you cry no more."

Songwriters: KERRY LIVGREN, KERRY A LIVGREN
© Sony/ATV Music Publishing LLC
For non-commercial use only

As I finish this story, I would be remiss if I did not tell you what I did with the lottery ticket winnings. At the time I was in the process of enrolling my daughter in a Lutheran parochial school. In order to do this, I needed a down payment of $500 for the tuition and book costs. The winning amount for getting 5 out of 6 numbers was exactly $500.

Now I can laugh because in hindsight I can see that God was providing a Bible-based education for my daughter and teaching me a lesson in faith, motives, situational importance, money and His ability to provide us with everything we *need* in this life. I emphasize **_need_** and not our fallen nature's **_greed_** that can so easily entangle us.

Two good Bible verses to end this lottery ticket story are:

> *Jeremiah 29:11-12* ^{*11*}*For I know the thoughts that I think toward you, says the L*ORD*, thoughts of peace and not of evil, to give you a future and a hope.* ^{*12*}*Then you will call upon Me and go and pray to Me, and I will listen to you.*

and

> *Hebrews 13:8* ^{*8*}*Jesus Christ is the same yesterday, today, and forever.*

The Second Lottery Ticket

As I write this second story about a lottery ticket, I should note that the date is now August 5, 2018. That makes it twenty years after I wrote the first story about the 1990s lottery ticket.

So, today I went into a grocery store, grabbed a shopping cart and decided to buy a $5 scratch off lottery ticket, little knowing that that would bring me to have another God encounter with the public.

I parked the cart in the first empty aisle that I found and began to scratch off the ticket to see if it was a winner or a loser. To my surprise, this $5 ticket had sixty bucks of winnings on it.

As I stood there beaming at my good fortune, I heard a voice behind me say, "Sir, can I help you find anything?" I turned around to face the voice addressing me to see a young twenty-something-year-old male in a store uniform. I smiled at the young clerk and told him I was finding what I needed but had stopped to scratch this lottery ticket. He got a big smile on his face and asked if it was a winner. With face aglow, I told him that I had just scored sixty bucks off a $5 ticket. He seemed more excited than I was as he asked if I wanted to split it with him.

We both laughed at his presumptuous gesture and I began telling him the previous story in this book that I called "Lottery Ticket." As I finished the tale I reached into my pocket and gave him a Chick Gospel tract named "Back From the Dead?" and told him that the story in that booklet was a well documented true story.

For a moment I shared with him my personal experience with God and told him how I had become a lay minister at about his age. And, that after being a Christian for over thirty-three years, I could attest to the fact that the information about God inside that little tract was verifiable truth. I encouraged him to read it and consider what it said.

Not wanting to occupy too much of his time, I grinned and said, "I'll tell you what. After I cash in this lottery ticket on my way out, I will buy another one. Who knows, it just may be a $100 winner. If it is, I will be generous and split it with you." We both laughed and I smiled at him as I walked away.

After I finished my shopping I cashed in the lottery ticket for the $60 winnings and bought another ticket before I left the store. I unloaded my purchases into the back seat of my vehicle and got in to drive away but before I started the vehicle, I grabbed the second lottery ticket and scratched it off to see if it was a winner or a loser.

To my utter amazement I saw that this ticket was a ONE HUNDRED DOLLAR WINNER! You just cannot make this stuff up! Instantly, the Holy Spirit reminded me of the last words I had spoken to that young store clerk.

I had told him that I would buy another lottery ticket on my way out of the store and, if it won $100, I WOULD SPLIT IT WITH HIM. Only for a moment did I think about reneging on those words but knowing that this was a Godly opportunity to impact this young man's life, I went back into the store.

The young man was still in the same aisle where I had left him. I approached him and asked, "Remember me?" He replied that he did and I asked him to come with me. As we walked to the front of the store, I asked him if he remembered the last words I had said to him. He answered that he did and quoted back to me, "If I win a hundred bucks on my way out of the store, I will split it with you."

We stopped in front of the lottery cash-out window. Then I held the winning ticket up close to him so he could read it. I asked, "How much does that say it's worth?" He smiled and said, "A hundred bucks" and I said, "That's right." Handing the ticket to the cashier, I asked for two fifty-dollar bills. I handed one to him and he reluctantly took it saying that I really did not have to do that for him. I asked him what he thought the odds were of my saying I would split a hundred dollar winning ticket with him and then it actually happened. He said, "Just about impossible."

Then I reminded him of that little pamphlet I had given him. "Only God," I said, "Could have pulled off those odds." I continued by saying, "It would seem that God is giving you fifty bucks to read that pamphlet and consider its content as there probably will be something in the near future that will require God's help in your life."

He agreed that only God could make that happen and assured me he would read the pamphlet. With a "God bless you" I left the store and proceeded home. I would be willing to wager that that young man will never forget our conversation and, hopefully, one day on heaven's side of eternity, I will learn what became of it.

Chapter 7

The Horse and Rider

Through the early morning mist, we see a lone white horse, trapped in a thicket of thorny bushes and dense brush. The horse is confused and lacks an escape route from his night wanderings in the dark.

He rears up on his hind legs trying to get a glimpse of a viable way out of his dilemma. The great white stallion attempts to kick and crash his way out of the thorny thicket but to no avail.

A man has heard the horse's frantic thrashing and heavy panting and he appears within the dense thicket. As he comes to the horse's aid he peacefully approaches the horse, that by now has fully entangled himself within the prison of the thorns.

In the shadowy light his calm voice speaks, "Easy now, big boy." He places a gentle hand on the side of the horse's face and strokes him all the way back to his mane for assurance. Then with his hand on the horse's mane, he leads the way through the brush into a clear and spacious opening.

In the semi-lit sky, the man, who now is also bloodied by the thorns on his forehead, hands, and feet, stands silently with the horse watching the dawning of a brand new day. They can see they must leave the barren land appearing before them. The man has already traveled on foot from a place far off but still has a long way to go.

The horse sees the man has no other companion and, in a gesture of gratitude, he kneels before him as an acknowledgement of transportation. The man strokes the great white stallion's coat and climbs aboard a submissive steed bought by the kindness of the man's rescuing work.

As we see the man, whom we will now call "the Rider," together with the grateful steed, it becomes apparent in the light of the early dawn that this is no ordinary man. He is clothed in royal attire, as one who is sent as an emissary to a foreign people. The rider wears a sword at his side and on his back he carries a large bag of scrolls, each one bearing the seal of a stately crown.

As they travel together, they come upon a village. The inhabitants quickly surround the white stallion and the royally attired rider who then loudly proclaims, "Hear Ye! Hear Ye" to all who have an ear with which to hear.

"A day is coming and now is near that will have you all fearfully running. For behind me is a great storm. A storm generated by an evil horde with intentions of conquering and conquest.

"Such a great evil in magnitude that no one who is not prepared will survive. The evil one comes in might and desires to smite. He will take your gold while he slays your old. His lips drip of honey as he steals your money."

The rider withdraws a scroll from the bag and states that there is a plan. "So, come one, come all, I beg you to heed my call." With his message spoken, the rider hands them a crown-crested scroll. "Read the scroll well," the rider instructs, "For it contains the words that will guide you out of your state."

The white stallion gallops away in full stride as the rider guides him down the trail. From village to village, they deliver the same message and leave a scroll at each location to guide the people to their rest. During their travels, they encounter thieves and robbers who wish to steal the crown-crested scrolls, but to their misfortune, the rider slides from his seat upon his trusted brave steed and wields his sword that yields their reward. Fall they do as the rider gallops through for he carries a message upon the steed's determined passage and together they work until all is fulfilled.

The Ambassador's Call

As the days pass we see that the rider stays strong to deliver his message. However, one day the great white steed slows from his gallop and collapses upon the ground. The faithful white horse as given all the strength that he has to offer for his mission of delivering the royally crested scrolls. His body heaves from the zealous gallop that he thought would please his rider and his cause. His once magnificent white coat is now bloodied and scarred from the battles with the thieves and robbers.

The horse thinks to himself, "I have fallen and failed my rider." With one last mighty burst of purpose-driven zeal, the horse attempts to stand once more. Alas, his spirit is willing, but his horseflesh has been weakened of all its strength. He cannot continue and he crashes down hard to the earth beneath him.

Gasping for breath, the horse tries to raise his head fully expecting to see the rider draw his sword to put him out of his misery for the horse recalls that many of his brothers have perished in that manner at the hands of former riders whom they served.

"This is tradition," he thinks. "My kind are meant to serve and then just fade away. When we are old, have fallen, or are deemed useless, then we are cast off or given to the sword." Closing his eyes, his head falls back into the dirt and he waits for the rider's sword to pierce his heart and his days to come to an end.

As he lies there in wait, he opens his eyes to gaze one last time upon the rider he has grown to love, but what is this? He widens his eyes and sees that the rider now kneels at his side. The rider bends down and presses his face into the side of the horse's face, as if to become one in shared agony. With his gentle hands now caressing the steed in solace, the rider looks deeply into his loyal friend's eyes. A tear runs from the great steed's eye and, as it traces down his cheekbone, it is joined by another tear, but this one is from the rider's eyes. The rider whispers these peaceful reassuring words into the steed's ear:

"My friend, today you will not die, for you are the apple of my eye. You carried me to the masses, so my message could save the last. You are my friend whom I deeply love. Together we fit as a well-tailored glove. In you I am well pleased, so you shall find your fear released."

Upon speaking these words, the rider gives his friend pure water to refresh him and food to nourish him. The rider lovingly applies a healing salve to the truehearted steed's wounds from bygone battles.

Then he leads his faithful friend to green pastures where he will regain his strength and to a stilled river of water where he may quench his thirst.

> ***Ezekiel 47:9** And it shall be that every living thing that moves, wherever the rivers go, will live. There will be a very great multitude of fish, because these waters go there; for they will be healed, and everything will live wherever the river goes.*

> ***Revelation 22:1-2** And he showed me a pure river of water of life, clear as crystal, proceeding from the throne of God and of the Lamb. ²In the middle of its street, and on either side of the river, was the tree of life, which bore twelve fruits, each tree yielding its fruit every month. The leaves of the tree were for the healing of the nations.*

The Allegory Explained

This allegory is dedicated to all who have been in Christian service during their lifetime.

In the beginning, we see the great white horse trapped within a cage of thorny bushes and brush that it finds inescapable. The white horse represents each one of us who has been called to Christian service and been lost in the thicket of indecision, reluctance, unbelief, or just plain wanting to pull a "Jonah" on our calling.

Jesus has a way of persuasion unlike any other. He will allow us to get caught up in our own self interests until we become entrapped in them. Like the rider, He waits in the distance until we have nowhere else to go.

When we are in our darkest place, Jesus comes, calms us and leads us into a spacious place. Once there, we spiritually see the bloody work that Jesus Himself suffered in order to come to our rescue. This is represented by the blood on the rider's hands, feet and forehead.

Once our hearts truly see and acknowledge His sacrifice for us personally, we are then willing to bend our knee in reverence towards Him in our calling to Christian service. When we do so, we realize the greatness and majesty of who Christ really is. Then, like the horse, we are able to invite Jesus to be our ever guiding and faithful Presence.

Our Initial Journey

One of the first places God led me in Christian service was to a homeless shelter. The people there were impoverished yet willing to listen. At the time two other lay brothers and I would take turns in sharing "The Golden Encrusted Scrolls" on Sundays to these meager and downtrodden people.

The "Golden Encrusted Scrolls," like in our allegory, is the saving message of the good news of the Gospel of Jesus Christ. God can use us as horses or ambassadors like we see in:

> ***Numbers 22:28** Then the LORD opened the donkey's mouth, and it said to Balaam, "What have I done to you to make you beat me these three times?" (NIV)*

God had me spend a couple years in this setting during which I received an ordination into the lay ministry. It is a special time in our lives when we feel like a purpose has been realized and a future made clear.

Through the Years

Through our years of Christian ministry many of us have been led to many places with each of them being an adventure of its own. However, I have found that many of the works God leads us into are for our own personal character development and can be most trying as Jesus noted in:

> *John 10:10-13 10The thief comes only to steal and kill and destroy; I have come that they may have life and have it to the full. 11"I am the Good Shepherd. The Good Shepherd lays down his life for the sheep. 12The hired hand is not the shepherd and does not own the sheep. So when he sees the wolf coming, he abandons the sheep and runs away. Then the wolf attacks the flock and scatters it. 13The man runs away because he is a hired hand and cares nothing for the sheep. (NIV)*

These verses are like our allegorical horse that endures the attacks of thieves and robbers along his journey. Oh, the untold times that many of us have suffered deception and outright lies from parishioners, close brethren, spiritual kin, and even from church leadership.

These kinds of attacks, and, yes, they **are** attacks, steal our sense of trust toward the ministry within Christendom and at times can leave us lacking in faith. Yet, hallelujah, we see in:

> *2 Timothy 2:10-13 10Therefore I endure all things for the sake of the elect, that they also may obtain the salvation which is in Christ Jesus with eternal glory. 11This is a faithful saying: for if we died with Him, we shall also live with Him. 12If we endure, we shall also reign with Him. If we deny Him, He also will deny us. 13If we are faithless, He remains faithful; He cannot deny Himself.*

Our Perceived Fall and Failures

During our service tour of duty, we can and have fallen into these mental traps of worthlessness, self-condemnation, and self judgement, to the point where we think that the Holy Spirit is not pleased with our current and historical work for the Gospel's cause.

Like our allegorical horse, we mentally, physically and emotionally crash into a state of uselessness. Remember we learned in:

> **Proverbs 13:12 *Hope deferred makes the heart sick, but when the desire comes, it is a tree of life.***

We hope that at that point our fellow brethren would come to our aid and give us comfort and encouragement. Yes, even financial relief if it is needed.

However, the phrase coined within Christendom is that "we are the best at killing our wounded." Who amongst us has not been guilty of pointing a finger at a supposed fallen believer like Sandi Patti, Michael English or Jimmy Swaggart? Most Christians were quick to gather around them like a Chicago gang, giving them a spiritual kicking fest while they were down.

The Rider's Rescue

It is at this point in many of our lives and, like our allegorical horse, we think Jesus is standing over us like a Saul of Tarsus, giving His approval of a Stephen being stoned. This is not the way of our Savior, our Lover, our Jesus. With Jesus, it is a matter of the heart and not of the flesh. God directs us to do this in our lives in:

> **Micah 6:8 *He has shown you, O man, what is good; and what does the LORD require of you but to do justly, to love mercy, and to walk humbly with your God?***

Then, would it not be reasonable to know that He would respond the same way during our time of need? Would our Jesus take His sword and finish us off like a horse in a western movie who gets a shot to the head after it falls? **NAY!!**

Scripture says the following in these situations:

> *Psalm 23:1-6 The Lord is my shepherd; I shall not want. ²He makes me to lie down in green pastures; He leads me beside the still waters. ³He restores my soul; He leads me in the paths of righteousness For His name's sake. ⁴Yea, though I walk through the valley of the shadow of death, I will fear no evil; For You are with me; Your rod and Your staff, they comfort me. ⁵You prepare a table before me in the presence of my enemies; You anoint my head with oil; My cup runs over. ⁶Surely goodness and mercy shall follow me All the days of my life; And I will dwell in the house of the Lord Forever.*
>
> *Psalm 50:15 Call upon Me in the day of trouble; I will deliver you, and you shall glorify Me."*
>
> *Revelation 21:4-7 ⁴"And God will wipe away every tear from their eyes; there shall be no more death, nor sorrow, nor crying. There shall be no more pain, for the former things have passed away." ⁵Then He who sat on the throne said, "Behold, I make all things new." And He said to me, "Write, for these words are true and faithful." ⁶And He said to me, "It is done! I am the Alpha and the Omega, the Beginning and the End. I will give of the fountain of the water of life freely to him who thirsts. ⁷He who overcomes shall inherit all things, and I will be his God and he shall be My son."*

Therefore, I will end this chapter with a Scripture verse for you who have run the race, endured the scourge and completed the task. No words can be of greater solace to you than these found in:

Matthew 25:23 His lord said to him, 'Well done, good and faithful servant; you have been faithful over a few things, I will make you ruler over many things. Enter into the joy of your lord.'

Gregory Addie

Chapter 8

The Train Station

It is very early morning. As the darkness of night gives way to dawn, the shape of an old train station is revealed. This station has existed since a time well before new creations of simplified travel automation were conceived in the minds of men. The station has faithfully served to provide shelter, destination logistics, redemption tickets, physical comfort and guidance during the long waiting times for each and every patron's departure.

The founders of this station have left several historic artifacts on the walls for visitors to view before they depart on their journey. On one wall inside a glass case are the three original spikes that were used to nail down the massive steel rails to the wood crossbeams for the train to travel upon. Under the glass case is a plaque of remembrance which reads, "In memory of all those who harshly died so that we may simplify travel."

On another wall is the original tall railroad clock with its gigantic face. Its hands have been maintained over time so that they still move to remind visitors of their upcoming time of departure. The station's creators have made this clock face exceptionally large so that all can see it from far off. In their wisdom the creators, who do not want anyone to miss their departing train due to a lack of discerning the correct time, have made the clock face numbers equally huge.

Also preserved within the building is the original ticket counter. It is still functional so that visitors can purchase redemption tickets from the ticket master as passage for their journey. Many a redemption ticket has been issued there over the years. Like a McDonald's hamburger sign, a sign over the ticket counter reads:

Welcome!
Millions of redemption tickets have been issued here.
Call out to the Ticket Master, and he will come
and make sure you receive your ticket.

The train that serves this station has not changed since the foundation was laid for the tracks. It still has the old wood-stoked steam engine. Its crew has not changed as well. A single sweaty old engineer works tirelessly to stoke the fires of the great engine for he knows that without his due diligence, the awaiting passengers may grow weary and possibly leave the station thereby missing their "final destination."

The remainder of the train's crew consists of a lone conductor. His job over the years has been to ensure that every passenger boarding the train has a validated redemption ticket which authorizes them to be on board. During the passenger's journey, the conductor provides refreshments and tentative arrival times for the passengers.

THE GATHERING

In this early dawn we begin to see a crowd of people gathering inside and outside of the train station. One can tell by their appearances that they are not of the same commonality. Every race appears to be represented amongst them as their skin colors range from yellow, black, and red to olive, tan and white. Their ethnic backgrounds are a diverse mix of Asian, African, Arab, American Indian, Middle Eastern, English, Norwegian, Scottish, Irish, Russian, German and the like.

Above the huge old clock, a new sign appears with unusual modern day flashing red lights. The sign blinks a marquee style message across its screen which reads:

The Ambassador's Call

"WELCOME! This message update is to inform you that this will be the LAST DEPARTURE from this station. All who wish to board the train for its final journey must acquire their redemption tickets NOW. We repeat. Your redemption tickets must be in hand before the train's departure time."

Upon reading this new information, many people panic and, thinking that they might miss the train, quickly scurry into line at the ticket office so they can obtain their redemption tickets.

Some are not so rushed and gather in small groups and reach the consensus that there is plenty of time to get their redemption tickets. "No rush needed" is heard amongst them. They simply stay gathered and talk about the worldly news of the day, not fully understanding that the time of the train's departure is close at hand.

Others see the long ticket line forming and leave the station thinking that "It's simply not worth the wait" or they reason that they will "Come back just before the train leaves." In their minds, this is like a baseball game where they can come sliding into home base at the last second and the umpire will call them "SAFE." Little do they realize that the ball is hurtling towards home much faster than their speed. The umpire will announce this group "OUT" while they are still running towards home plate.

Still another group of people leaves the station thinking, "Ah – just another sales gimmick. This station is not closing. I'll bet it will still be selling its promised rides for another 100 years." This group simply never returns to the station.

Just beyond the train station is a pond that the station's creators designed to be a place where passengers can sit and ponder their upcoming journey. On the crest of a hill to the east of the pond are three ornamental ten-foot sections of train track rails rising up out of the earth. Lying horizontally across the top of these rails is an old wooden crossbeam dripping with cobwebs accumulated from many years of stagnation.

Finally, we see one last group of people outside the station clustered around the pond. Many of them are contemplating entering the train station but feel they are too low class to ride the last train. Surely, the wealthy and prominent will acquire the remaining seats before an opportunity presents itself to *them*.

Many of those now near the pond come closer to the water's edge and peer down into the dark water. There is just enough glimmer of light from the dawn that they can see deep enough into the pond's shallow water to observe the secrets lying on the bottom. There in their own private graveyard are heaps of old bottles, rusty cans, fish skeletons and other forms of garbage polluting this once serene place of contemplation.

The people think to themselves that the filthy bottom of this pond is just like their lives have been. Shallow. Darkened. Full of garbage, doubt and low self-worth.

However, none of these people have done their research. They do not understand that these redemption tickets have been prepaid for *every* person who will simply come and accept a ticket. They have failed to properly read the disclosure statement of this station's history in that, since its inception, **ALL** tickets have been prepaid for **ALL** regardless of social position or wealth.

Suddenly, this group's dark self-reflections are interrupted by the piercing first shaft of sunlight as the golden orb peeks over the eastern hill. The sun continues its climb into the sky and the old rails and wooden crossbeam become illuminated and are set aglow by the old cobwebs' dispersion of the light. The pond slowly becomes a golden mirror of stillness and peace. As this metamorphosis occurs, the people realize they can no longer see the garbage on the bottom but only a perfect reflection of the shadow of the rails and cross beam spilling across the water like a biblical cross. **THE CROSS**. Hope for a better life in the future begins to fill their minds.

Like a gift from the heavens, their hearts are enlightened by a new revelation through the creators' foreknowledge and wisdom of placing this simple representation near the station and the pond. They turn with a sense of renewed worth toward the ticket line which now extends out of the station. The ticket master begins to announce that the train's arrival is fast approaching.

He calls out in a loud voice, **"Last call for your redemption tickets!"** as he proceeds to the ticket counter. He yells a second warning, **"Please remember, there will be NO entry onto the train without a validated redemption ticket!"**

Heeding his call, the people at the pond "who understand the time is now at hand" immediately get into the line and receive their redemption tickets at no charge.

Outside of the station the crowd of people begin to see what appears to be a "growing cloud of smoke" far down the tracks and just around the bend. Excitement begins to spread amongst the people as they anticipate the imminent arrival of the train.

THE ARRIVAL

The train now begins to make its appearance on the horizon. From its metal belly billows smoke and steam which encompass the train in a thick cloud as it slowly approaches the station. A whistle blast, much like the sound of a mighty trumpet, seems to split the cloud of steam as the ticket master announces the train's final approach.

As the train draws nearer, we can see that it is pulling an endless number of passenger cars that stretch as far as the eye can see. The smoke and steam begin to dissipate as the train slowly comes into view becoming a clearer picture of what the passengers had expected to see.

With one last mighty blast of the whistle, the engineer brings the train to a complete stop in front of the train station. The crowd swells towards the departure gate anxiously awaiting the conductor's admittance.

The conductor carefully begins to open the train's passenger doors. When they are open wide he steps off the train and proceeds toward the departure gate with a pad of *RED* ink and a validation stamp in hand. *"Single file please,"* he announces as he positions himself at the gate which is very narrow and designed so that all who enter through it must face the conductor. As the people press forward the conductor cries out to the crowd with a welcoming smile, *"Please have your redemption ticket in hand as you enter the gate."*

The ticket master comes out of the station and hands the conductor a book which lists all those who have acquired their as yet unvalidated redemption tickets prior to the train's arrival. Without being noticed, he quietly slips aboard the train.

The conductor takes the book and begins to carefully compare each person's redemption ticket with the names in the book. As he verifies each person's name they hand over their redemption ticket and he stamps it with his final approval stamp in large red letters. Once approved, each individual proceeds through the gate and boards the train to await its departure.

As the conductor is processing the tickets, he begins to encounter a variety of people attempting to pass through the gate without a ticket. The first to try is an elderly couple. The elderly lady hands the conductor a redemption ticket, her name is verified, her ticket stamped and she is allowed to pass through the gate. Her husband attempts to pass through the gate closely behind her and is stopped abruptly by the conductor who says, *"Sir, your ticket please."* The elderly gentleman looks baffled as he explains to the conductor that he thought his wife's ticket covered them both.

The conductor says sadly, *"I'm sorry, Sir. Each person must have **their own ticket** to pass through this gate."* When the man cannot produce his own ticket, the conductor says, *"Sir, please depart from the line."*

The next party the conductor meets is a religious group led by their pastor. The pastor, exhibiting his good manners, allows his congregation to go ahead of him. Most of them have a redemption ticket but a few have failed to heed the pastor's messages about getting to the station on time and have not procured their own ticket.

The names of these few are not found in the ticket master's book and they too are asked to step out of the line. The pastor is dismayed that they will not all be traveling together, but he presents his ticket which is verified and stamped and he proceeds through the gate as the conductor comments, *"Well done. You have waited a long time for this trip. Enjoy your journey."*

The rest of the rejected church group begin to rail at the conductor, *"Hey! We have been with our pastor from the beginning. We thought we could enter through the gate on his ticket."* *" I am so sorry,"* the conductor replies. *"But only those who have their own redemption ticket and are recorded in this book are allowed through the gate. Your names are not listed here."*

In a panic, the church group, along with several other groups of people, rush back into the train station to attempt to acquire their own redemption tickets. To their utter dismay the ticket master has closed the redemption ticket office and has placed a sign on the door that reads, **"Closed. No more tickets are available for this trip!!"**

The crowd knocks and pounds on the office door, yelling in hopes that the ticket master would once again open the door and issue the redemption tickets needed for them to pass through the conductor's gate. Alas, like in biblical Noah's day, the door remains shut and their cries go unheeded.

Near the end of the long line are groups of people who knew that the train would be coming but were either too impatient to wait in line at the ticket office, or had made other plans for this day and then took too long to arrive once they heard the train was coming, or simply thought that they could purchase their redemption ticket as they attempted to enter the departure gate as if they were going through the drive thru at a fast food restaurant. Each of them was turned away as their name was not found in the ticket master's book.

THE DEPARTURE

Having now accounted for all the redemption tickets which matched the names in the book, the conductor turns, closes the departure gate behind him, boards the train and seals the passenger doors. He calls out to the engineer, "All Aboard!" As the engineer throttles the train forward, again a cloud of steam fills the air and the train slips down the old rugged tracks in the same manner as it had arrived.

The ticket master and the conductor come to the engineer and begin to discuss the train's last journey. The ticket master smiles at the other two and says, "Wow! You were really ahead of schedule for this last trip."

The engineer said that he wanted it to be this way as he knew that those waiting at the station had been expecting the day of his arrival for a very long time. He smiled and said, "Everyone hates a latecomer, but everyone loves it and is surprised when they find they did not have to wait as long as they thought they would."

With that said the train slowly disappears into the engine's cloud of steam and off into the future. As the train's long heavy load bears down onto the tracks, one can almost hear the spikes and rails which are fastened to the old wooden crossbeams cry out with a loud joyous squeal.

The End Is Just The Beginning

Dear reader, throughout this book I have shared several allegorical stories with you and given you insights into each for your understanding and edification.

In the Bible we see these words from Jesus Christ Himself, ***"He who has ears to hear, let him hear what the Spirit says."*** We see this in:

> *Mark 4:1-9 Again Jesus began to teach by the lake. The crowd that gathered around Him was so large that He got into a boat*

and sat in it out on the lake, while all the people were along the shore at the water's edge. ²He taught them many things by parables, and in His teaching said: ³"Listen! A farmer went out to sow his seed. ⁴As he was scattering the seed, some fell along the path, and the birds came and ate it up. ⁵Some fell on rocky places, where it did not have much soil. It sprang up quickly, because the soil was shallow. ⁶But when the sun came up, the plants were scorched, and they withered because they had no root. ⁷Other seed fell among thorns, which grew up and choked the plants, so that they did not bear grain. ⁸Still other seed fell on good soil. It came up, grew and produced a crop, some multiplying thirty, some sixty, some a hundred times." ⁹Then Jesus said, "<u>Whoever has ears to hear, let them hear.</u>" (NIV)

Mark 4:21-23 ²¹He said to them, "Do you bring in a lamp to put it under a bowl or a bed? Instead, don't you put it on its stand? ²²For whatever is hidden is meant to be disclosed, and whatever is concealed is meant to be brought out into the open. ²³If anyone has ears to hear, let them hear." (NIV)

Luke 14: 28-35 ²⁸ "Suppose one of you wants to build a tower. Won't you first sit down and estimate the cost to see if you have enough money to complete it? ²⁹For if you lay the foundation and are not able to finish it, everyone who sees it will ridicule you, ³⁰saying, 'This person began to build and wasn't able to finish.' ³¹"Or suppose a king is about to go to war against another king. Won't he first sit down and consider whether he is able with ten thousand men to oppose the one coming against him with twenty thousand? ³²If he is not able, he will send a delegation while the other is still a long way off and will ask for terms of peace. ³³In the same way, those of you who do not give up everything you have cannot be my disciples. ³⁴"Salt is good, but if it loses its saltiness, how can it be made salty again? ³⁵It *is fit neither for the soil nor for the manure pile; it is thrown out. (NIV)*

"Whoever has ears to hear, let them hear."

Revelation 2:7 <u>Whoever has ears, let them hear what the Spirit says</u> to the churches. To the one who is victorious, I will give the right to eat from the tree of life, which is in the paradise of God. (NIV) (emphasis mine)

Revelation 2:11 <u>Whoever has ears, let them hear what the Spirit says</u> to the churches. The one who is victorious will not be hurt at all by the second death. (NIV) (emphasis mine)

Revelation 2:17 <u>Whoever has ears, let them hear what the Spirit says</u> to the churches. To the one who is victorious, I will give some of the hidden manna. I will also give that person a white stone with a new name written on it, known only to the one who receives it. (NIV) (emphasis mine)

Revelation 2:26-29 ²⁶To the one who is victorious and does My will to the end, I will give authority over the nations — ²⁷that one 'will rule them with an iron scepter and will dash them to pieces like pottery'—just as I have received authority from My Father. ²⁸I will also give that one the morning star. ²⁹ <u>Whoever has ears, let them hear what the Spirit says</u> to the churches. (emphasis mine)

In all these different passages, Jesus wants the reader to think deeply upon what He said or what the disciples had written of how they witnessed His message.

The story of "The Train Station" will be no different now that we are at the end of our book. Please take the time to read and re-read that story and ASK the Holy Spirit to guide you to its full meaning and conclusion.

As a partial help to your endeavor, I will tell you that this story is an allegory about eternal salvation and the means to obtain it.

The main cast in this story is made up of:

- *The TICKET MASTER who is THE HOLY SPIRIT;*
- *The CONDUCTOR who is JESUS CHRIST;*
- *The ENGINEER who is GOD, OUR HEAVENLY FATHER;*
- *and*
- *The REDEMPTION TICKET is HOW YOU GET TO BOARD THE TRAIN INTO ETERNAL LIFE.*

With that said, I invite everyone who has read this book, and doubts their eternal security, to pray this prayer right now:

A SALVATION PRAYER

Heavenly Father, I call upon you in the name of your Son Jesus Christ.

I ask and receive Jesus and His sacrifice for my sins, especially the sin of unbelief concerning Jesus Christ.

I confess and believe that Jesus Christ died on a cross and rose from the grave to provide payment for my eternal SALVATION.

Fill me now with the Holy Spirit, that I may understand your gift of eternal life.

I agree according to Matthew 18:19 and with the person who wrote this book that in the following days You will, in your way, confirm this prayer.

In Jesus' name, Amen

Please read *John 3:16-18* and *Romans 10:13*. May God bless your life richly.

Gregory Addie

Future Writings in the Works

The Wheat Field – A harvesting of hearts

The Traveler – A perfect reflection

The Apple Tree – A Springtime's blossom

Mother Earth's Womb – Another look at abortion

Contact: addiegregory52@gmail.com

Gregory Addie is available for book interviews and personal appearances. For more information contact:

Gregory Addie
C/O Advantage Books
P.O. Box 160847
Altamonte Springs, FL 32716
info@advbooks.com

To purchase additional copies of this book visit our bookstore website at:
www.advbookstore.com

Longwood, Florida, USA
"we bring dreams to life"™
www.advbookstore.com

www.ingramcontent.com/pod-product-compliance
Lightning Source LLC
LaVergne TN
LVHW051130080426
835510LV00018B/2324